Three Days Running

The Revised Autobiography of

Sheila Willcox
© *1958 Estate of Sheila Willcox*

Introduction by Cate Bryant
© *2018 Cate Bryant*

Epona Publishing

Dedicated to

My parents, and also to Chips to whom I owed it all.

Table of Contents

Chapter One - My Folly 6
Chapter Two – Ponies Galore 19
Chapter Three – Blithe Spirit 28
Chapter Four – A Partnership Begins 34
Chapter Five – Meeting the Stars 50
Chapter Six – Swiss Venture 54
Chapter Seven – Riding Cross-Country 58
Chapter Nine – European Championships 73
Chapter Ten – Losing Chips 90
Chapter Eleven – Stockholm Olympics, 1956 108
Chapter Twelve – The Partnership Resumed 114
Chapter Thirteen – Harewood, 1956 122
Chapter Fourteen – Becoming Famous 136
Chapter Fifteen – A Marriage Proposal 143
Chapter Sixteen – Badminton, 1957 148
Chapter Seventeen – Riding for England 161
Chapter Eighteen – Jumping for Gold 175
Chapter Nineteen – My Broken Heart 187
Chapter Twenty – True Love 203
Chapter Twenty-One – Wedding Bells 210

Introduction

Three Days Running was first published in 1958. It was the autobiography of Sheila Willcox for the first twenty-two years of her life. It was the story of Britain's foremost all-round horsewoman, who leapt to the top of the eventing world on her horse High and Mighty in an almost unbelievable space of time. Eventing has been described as the most demanding competition for horse and rider and was originally confined to the military. But in the 1950s more and more women were to come forward to challenge men at their own game. Sheila Willcox and High and Mighty won many spectacular victories both in England and abroad and this highlighted the illogical and contentious rule that women were excluded from competing in Olympic three-day eventing.

Sheila was born on the outskirts of Birmingham. With the coming of WWII, her family moved north to settle on the coast of Lancashire. She learnt to ride on the ponies on the beach and then acquired her first pony, Folly. During her teenage years she competed in local shows in showing events, show jumping and gymkhana games. Her debut into the adult world at seventeen was with the show hack Blithe Spirit and she won Supreme Champion Hack at the White City Royal International Horse Show.

She then decided to compete in what was known then as horse trials, now known as three-day eventing. She bought Chips, whose competition name was High and Mighty, and they won every major competition in sight. In 1956 they came a close second to Colonel Frank Weldon riding Kilbarry at Badminton, under very questionable conditions. In the following year she won, again riding High and Mighty.

The original version of *Three Days Running* finished after her first win at Badminton and her gold medal in Copenhagen. In this revised edition I have included many details that were omitted from the original publication and gone on to describe her second Badminton win and her marriage to John Waddington in November of that year. Sheila died after being ill with Alzheimer's in 2017. Her family have decided that 20 per cent of the profits from the e-publication of her books will go towards an Alzheimer's charity. She left behind voluminous manuscripts detailing many aspects of her life. I have incorporated some of this extra material into this book, including the way in which she was seduced by a man prominent in the eventing world at that time, and how this affected the rest of her life. I have also extended the time-line until November 1958.

Sheila was not an easy person to understand. With great talent perhaps comes eccentricities and sometimes in her dealings with people she was unbending. She was self-centred and single-minded but above all else she loved horses. Perhaps in her relationships with horses she excelled because she would dominate them and when they submitted to her will, they loved her and could be trained to the highest levels.

There are also more detailed accounts of the way in which she trained her horses and rode cross-country courses. If read in conjunction with *The Event Horse* (published by Epona Publishing and available through Amazon) you can learn much about every aspect of training for, and competing in one-day events and three-day events.

Sheila was a very strong character and she went her own way, but there is no denying that she was probably one of the most gifted horse riders and trainers of the twentieth century. Mary King paid tribute to Sheila in her own autobiography which was published in 2009, with Chapter Three entitled 'The Sheila Willcox Years'. Mary says that she learnt more from Sheila Willcox than any other single person and this is perhaps one of Sheila's greatest legacies.

Chapter One - My Folly

I was ten years old when I first set eyes on Folly: a mane-tossing, eighteen-month-old scrap of a bay pony, flying delightedly across a field at the whistle of her owner-breeder, galloping into our lives – and changing the course of mine completely. Our excursions into the horse world had always been 'a bit of a lark', but during my late teens they took on an aura of fantasy. For our family background was entirely suburban, based on business and academic careers and given to rugger, tennis, golf and bridge-playing, by way of weekend relaxation. No history of horsey connections anywhere, so if I was a throw-back, I had been thrown back a long way.

I was born on 12th March, 1936, at Sutton Coldfield, near Birmingham. Had it not been for the war I would, no doubt, have stayed there and followed the family pattern, but as my father's business took him all over the British Isles, there was therefore no need for us to suffer the nightly German air-raids. My parents decided it was idiotic to carry two babies up and down from the shelter in the garden, every night, so, between a winter's dawn and the evening wail of the siren, they rushed to Lytham, in Lancashire to look at houses my father had quickly picked out from a list.

We moved to Lytham, but we had not meant to stay. Both my brother John and I went to schools in the Midlands, and my parents were always going off to look at houses in those counties, never finding the right one. A good thing too, for John and I had a wonderful childhood there. It was a small place – Americans stationed just outside used to refer to our main street as "the little shops in the trees"; and about our weather they would say, "When we can see Blackpool Tower, it's going to rain. When we can't, it is raining". Up to the war strangers coming to live at Lytham were known as 'off-comers', and almost had to serve the Biblical seven years before being accepted into the fold. It was soaked in the history of the Clifton family whose home and estate played a major part in my story. Everybody spoke to everybody, irrespective of position or calling; the tradespeople still treated the customer as if he or she was right; the buses waited if the driver saw one running; and everybody joined in their neighbours' moments of happiness, and helped in adversity. All of which made for an 'air', and I for one, wouldn't have lived in a city for all the tea in China. Lytham was only half the borough, the other half was St. Annes, a more sophisticated and fashionable holiday resort, where the beautiful sands began, rolling for miles to Blackpool. And this was where my life with horses started.

In the summer we had a chalet on the beach. Until John and I went to school, most of every fine day was spent there. Naturally enough we made friends with the riding stable proprietors, who took down ponies every day during the season. I expect there were a good many sixpenny rides before I came off the leading rein, but soon I was begging to be allowed to ride to the beach with the Lytham ponies, instead of being taken there on a bicycle or in the little half-hourly bus – petrol was rationed in those days. Presently I was promoted to leading the sixpenny rides and felt very superior to the greenhorns who couldn't even bump! Which brings me to one of the many family stories my father told, being one of those rare, enviable people who could make a joke against himself.

In those days my father couldn't often spare the time to be with us on the beach, but this occasion must have been a holiday. My brother and I teased him into coming for a ride, never dreaming that anything on four legs could present difficulties to such a wizard with things on four wheels. He scornfully refused the offer of a leading rein, and off we started on the longest itinerated ride to the breakwater, half a mile away. All went well - apart from the understandable discomfort to a non-rider, most unsuitably dressed, on an un-mouthed, one-track-minded bony quadruped, until we were about to turn for home. At that moment, the officer in charge of a gun-battery, somewhere in the dunes beyond, chose to give the signal to fire. The ponies' whirl round wouldn't have disgraced an Arab desert patrol, and we had the fastest ride on record back to the home stand. My father stayed on – he said because he was too heavy to be dislodged - and having cautiously grounded himself and got his breath, said proudly to my brother, "What did you think of that, John?" To which John, not wishing to hurt anybody's feelings, replied, "Well, your face is red, Daddy." Later, in more adult company, my father added ruefully, "If it had only been my face that had been red!" He had been sitting on the reins the whole time.

During the winter we could hire the Lytham ponies by the hour. As trade was slack, I got much more than my five shillings' worth, for the stable girl had a lot of exercising to do. The proprietor was an old man of eighty, quite illiterate, but smart enough to have made secure his old age and his family's future. He was a local character, with his finger in a good many pies, and knew a lot about horses. No vet could hope for much business from his stables. I watched and learnt, and found much wisdom in his dialect-embroidered sayings.

And so, to Folly – careering madly across a paddock and slithering to a stop to nibble at a hand-held bun. All her life she would eat anything, and her nickname of 'the dustbin' illustrated perfectly her capabilities. She had enchanted us. The day I first met her had been a miserable one, for I was ten years old and the sentence of boarding-school at Haunton had been passed on me some time ago. Haunton itself was a delightful place, even on that grey soaking-wet day, but the thought of leaving home made me feel as brooding as the skies above.

We were staying at Ashby, and there was a country fair-cum-market in progress just across the road from our hotel. When we returned for lunch, we saw a small pony under a tree – heavy raindrops dripping on its unprotected quarters. It looked as miserable as I felt. Two of us, I thought, it for sale and I for school – we'll go together; and we would have bought it there and then, but for the fact that the owner was nowhere to be found. The hotel Boots (man who worked in the hotel) had been watching our antics. Finally, he came across to assure us that we certainly didn't want that poor beast, but he had a little beauty playing with her dam in the field at the back of the hotel; why didn't we take a look at her? The rain stopped as we followed him, and the sun came out as Folly galloped into our lives.

We called her Folly because, after we got her home, we were made to realise by kindly disposed advisors just how foolish it was to buy an eighteen-month-old filly for riding. What fun and games we had as I carried out the breaking-in process.

I decided that I would break her in and ride her by myself. All I knew was what I had seen in films when the cowboy hero would have his horse tied to a large post in the open and then approach him or her carrying the saddle, and a saddle-blanket which was placed underneath to stop it from rubbing the horse's back. All I had was a bridle without a noseband, and a hemp halter and rope. The cowboy's method was to leave the saddle to one side and begin to flap the blanket at the horse from a distance of a few feet, starting on one side and working nearer all the way round. If the horse accepted this without shying away, the next step was to place the saddle-blanket on his or her back, then the saddle with the girth pulled tight, and, hey presto, the cowboy jumped up on to the horse and galloped off into the sunset. I did not think that Folly would co-operate to the extent that all this would be completed within a few minutes, which was all the time it took in films, but luckily, I had no saddle so we did not have to worry about that part.

By great good fortune Daddy had recently replaced the green baize cover on his billiard table and he was happy to give me a large piece of this when I suggested that I could use it as a saddle. I folded it into a neat oblong shape and thought that it would be soft and comfortable for both of us. I needed something to keep it in place and asked Mummy if I could have some of her old washing line to act as a girth. I was ready to begin.

As soon as I started to put on her bridle the cows became extremely interested. They surrounded us, and there was a lot of vocal mooing and pushing. All our friends had been aware that this was the big day for me to get on Folly for the first time and they had arrived at the field, especially to witness the occasion. They took up vantage points perched along the field's nearest post-and-rail fence. When it became clear that I would not be able to manage our objective with a herd of cows also taking part, they had to get down from their perches and wait for me to lead Folly up to the top of the field where there was a gate, open it to get out and carefully close it again to be sure none of the cows followed us.

Folly and I, now minus cows, walked happily back towards Mythop Road on the dirt track and turned into our garage forecourt. This time the audience settled on the surrounding red brick wall.

Folly loved people. She had soon discovered that they gave her apples and sugar and sometimes sweets. She happily accepted everything on offer. We stood her in the middle of the forecourt over the drain, and I handed over the bridle reins to my brother John to hold her while I prepared myself with the green baize. I asked John if he was ready and he said yes. I talked to Folly and began to flap our 'saddle'. She was nuzzling John in the hope that he had something for her to eat and took not the slightest notice. The audience was getting bored. I walked more purposefully towards her and she looked at me as if to say, 'What on earth are you doing?' and continued to concentrate on John's pockets. I flapped the green baize as if it were a pillow case in the wind all round her in a circle, and came to the conclusion that it did not bother her in the least.

John stood in front of her as I approached and let her feel the touch of the baize on her nose. Then I moved to her nearside, the left, and stroked her. She turned her head as if to say, 'carry on', and I placed the saddle on her back. No reaction. I took the washing line and began to feed it over the baize. She did not care so I began to tighten it, making sure the knot would not lie against her coat. There she stood, saddle and bridle on, and not the slightest objection. I walked her round and she acted as if she had one of these on every day. It was time for me to get on. None of the onlookers knew how to give a leg up properly so I decided I would have to get on her from the top of the red brick wall, and one side of the wall was cleared of spectators so that I could climb aboard.

Then John brought her sideways on to me and I talked to her and stroked her and then put some weight on her by leaning over. Once again, she took no notice. I decided it was time to get on and with a little bounce off the wall, jumped into the 'saddle'. Folly tensed and turned her head. I told her what a good girl she was, and she immediately relaxed. That was enough for the first day, but I knew that the audience was disappointed that she had not turned into a bucking bronco and thrown me off. There was always a next time.

During the following months Folly's education continued apace. Every day I would saddle her up with the green baize and take her into the field around the corner, accompanied by friends who had nothing better to do, and there was always the possibility that I might provide real entertainment by falling off. From time to time she would get bored with me teaching her to answer my instructions, 'aids' in horsey language, and either stop so suddenly that I shot off the front, or waited until an argument was going on with the circle of onlookers, none of whom were horsey, about how we should proceed in the training. She would suddenly jump forward and give a large buck, which scattered us effectively. She would then hightail it to the gate, and disappear back to her field.

My mother would hear her flying hoofs, drop whatever she happened to be doing, mount a bicycle and – having first counted whole heads among the breakers-in – would pedal furiously to the field, where almost invariably Folly would be waiting to be let in.

Mummy realised that I needed a saddle to help me stay on board and had a word with Daddy, and we found a saddler who came to measure Folly over her withers and the shape of her back. Within days she had a smart leather saddle with stirrups, leathers and proper girths to replace Daddy's baize and Mummy's washing line. I felt a lot more secure and that was the end of Folly's dashes for freedom.

One of Ernie Eccleston's girls, who worked for him looking after the beach ponies at his stables behind the Railway Hotel, asked me if I was going to compete at the Lytham Agricultural Show in August. I had not thought of this and was told by Mr Eccleston that there would be show classes for ponies and that Folly would be eligible for the smallest height class, 'not exceeding 12.2 hands high'. That I would have to have a velvet riding hat, a shirt and tie and a proper riding coat and jodhpurs with riding boots and string gloves, and I would have to train Folly to give a little show in front of the judge. I explained all this to Mummy and Daddy. My Christmas presents were moved forward, and I even had two pairs of jods so that I always had a clean pair ready. I looked after Folly's saddle and bridle, cleaning and polishing it after every training session or ride, and my tan jodhpur boots with their elastic sides shone like conkers. I was very proud, and very determined not to let Mummy and Daddy down.

I sent for a schedule of events from the Show Secretary and avidly went through the list of classes for horses and ponies as soon as it arrived through the post. I saw that there was a class for two-year-olds in hand. Mr Eccleston had not mentioned that I would have two classes, so I had to practise running her up on foot to show how she moved at the walk and trot. All my helpers acted as judges to ensure that Folly and I kept to a straight line, going away from the judges at the walk, and back towards them at the trot.

In the 12.2 h.h. showing class the competitors would ride round the show arena first at the walk, then at the trot, and then at the canter. The judge would ask his steward to pull in the riders in order of merit and stand them in a line. He would inspect each pony at close quarters to see if they were sound, no lumps or bumps on their legs, lastly open their mouths to look at their teeth to see how old they were. After the inspection he would send out each partnership to give an individual show, to include a figure of eight at the canter, leading with left leg when going to the left, and with the right leg when going to the right. I could see that Folly and I had a lot to learn!

A letter arrived soon after I had filled in my entry form for the two classes. It was from a horror-stricken Secretary, who pointed out that the two-year-old class was for heavy horses only. I was mortified at my mistake, but consoled myself that now we could concentrate on the showing class.

I needed to understand how a horse or pony 'led' with one leg or the other at the canter. I watched Folly in the field and organised two or three of our friends to chase her round so that I could see which leg was leading at the canter. I needed to be quick at spotting what happened with Folly's legs as my helpers were not keen on all this fast running to keep her going, but with eyes slitted in concentration I managed to register that a canter stride was in three-time, first a hind leg started it, next the diagonal hind-leg and foreleg together, and thirdly, the remaining front leg – the leading leg. If the horse or pony was balanced properly, he or she would be leading with the right front leg, the off-fore, when cantering to the right, and with the left front leg, the near-fore, when cantering to the left.

I found out from Mr Eccleston that the show classes always went to the right for the first walk, trot and canter around the arena, and that I should try to make sure that the judge could see me, not allow another competitor to 'cover me up'. Folly and I had to learn together. I began to work her in the middle of the field and would trot her fast up a straight line and then, using my right rein turn her to the right, kicked her hard to move into canter. I would then look down to see if her right front leg was leading and if it was, I would make a big fuss of her and give her a lump of sugar. In this way she learnt to canter to left or right with the correct leg leading.

As the big day approached, I cycled down Park View Road, round the number 4 bus stop, and turned in past the Lodge and up the drive leading to the Clifton Estate's Home Farm. The show was held all over the first big field. Already the main arena, where Folly and I were due to make our debut, was roped in, and there were tents in all directions. There were sections marked Shire Horses which I might have joined had the secretary not seen my entry mistake, another for sheep, one for cows and another for Sheep Dog Trials. It was all very exciting. I went home and saddled up Folly so that she could have a quick look and lessen the shock of the next day. I do not think she realised the significance of what was in store, our debut into competition, but she was getting used to humans doing peculiar things. That afternoon I washed her mane and tail, and gave her a thorough grooming, first with my dandy brush – a strong bristled one, then with the body brush, softer, to smooth her coat and make her shine, and lastly with one of Mummy's big dusters to polish her off. I told her not to get dirty in the field and went home to get all my own clothes ready for the morning. I was beside myself with the excitement of it all.

The big day dawned, and it was lovely and sunny. We were lucky. I was up early to collect Folly from the field and bring her into the garage to check that she had not rolled in any cow muck. I cleaned out her feet with the hoof pick and scrubbed out each of them with one of Mummy's old floor brushes and warm water, finishing off with a drying cloth and a final coat of black Kiwi shoe polish on the outside. I kept talking to her to let her know what we were doing today and how well she must behave in the ring. Daddy minded her for me while I went to change into my best clothes and Mummy made me sit whilst she combed back my blonde hair and plaited it neatly with a large ribbon and each plait ending in a yellow bow. This turnout for hair continued for the rest of my participation in the showing, jumping and gymkhana classes of my juvenile years.

Then I was on Folly's back and setting off for the showground. It had not entered my head that we should win a prize, but to wear a number, to be called by name into the ring and to walk, trot and canter round with other competitors – just like in the pony books - that would be absolute bliss. Folly and I were both total novices at the game. I knew we had a lot to learn, but all we could do was our best. What I really wanted was to feel what it was like to ride a show pony in the ring, and I was intent on learning as much as I could in the process.

When we reached the lodge gates there were cars driving in and showing their passes to the official standing in the wooden box by the gate into the show field. He saw me coming and stopped a car. With a broad smile, he waved me on so that I could pass straight through the gateway into the field. I did not recognise him, but I expect he was one of Daddy's friends from the Green Drive Golf Club. No doubt my father had been telling them, ad infinitum, that his daughter was competing at the show. There were horseboxes trundling in and I was ready for Folly to have a fit. Amazingly, she took no notice, she was probably shell-shocked, and we arrived outside the main arena without a mishap.

An old man, with a knowledgeable gleam in his eye, looked at us and said, "You can't go into the ring like that."

"Why not?" said my father, all belligerent.

"Well," said the old man. "The pony's mane should be plaited."

I looked with alarm at the smart hair-dos of the other children's mounts, and my heart sank. "Never mind," said the man. "We'll hog it." Before our eyes he produced a large pair of scissors and proceeded to shave away what little mane there was. This performance must have put Folly into a trance, for she behaved like a veteran in the class. She was pulled in third, and finished second when number two disgraced himself by playing the bucking bronco. So, I won my first rosette. No other award has ever thrilled me so much, and at the same time I was determined that no matter which branch of equestrianism I should eventually take up, I should strive to emulate the leaders.

That autumn Folly and I both went to school, most unwillingly. Because of petrol rationing we had to go by train. I insisted on riding in the groom's compartment, a nightmare of a journey for my mother, who tells of how she set out in her best hat and fox furs and arrived looking like a harvest festival.

The riding teacher, Miss Grainger, turned out to have stables at her house some miles away and kept several show ponies. She watched me with Folly and decided that I would be good enough, with some guidance from her, to ride these for her in the ring. She asked Sister Patrice for permission to take me out of school on Saturdays to go to the shows, and I had a wonderful time riding in the 12.2 h.h. and 13.2 h.h. classes. She showed me how to plait the ponies' manes, trim the 'feathers' from the heels, and the long hairs from the face and ears. I watched and learned as she pulled their tails at the top to produce the professional smooth touch required for a real show horse or pony in the ring. I was lucky indeed to have this opportunity to learn, and I absorbed everything.

In the winter of 1947, we all woke up one morning to find it had been snowing hard in the night and was already several inches thick. Naturally, we pupils were thrilled and shot outside at our first break in lessons to throw snowballs at each other and build snowmen. It began to pall when the snow continued to float down and formed first a carpet, then a mattress and grew so high that it was too deep for us to go outside. The drive had to be kept clear for access to the country road outside and the men from the convent's farm were detailed to make sure that we were not totally cut off.

Folly caught strangles, a very nasty disease affecting her throat, which is not only very dangerous but also truly revolting with its thick yellow matter issuing forth. She took it very badly and lay at death's door for several weeks. Eventually, she was fit enough to be invalided home, and at this stage the snow had been shovelled every day to the sides of the roads until it was more than twelve feet high. Daddy arrived in his car and was met by a local man with a horsebox for hire ready to take Folly back to Lytham. I went with Daddy in the car and it was quite amazing driving along the road, with packed snow towering over us, more than twice the height of the car, and frozen into glacier-like walls whose brightness dazzled my eyes.

Once we got Folly home, I decided that she should never again go to school. So now at the end of the holidays, farewells to Folly had always to be said – and how heart-breaking they were. Tears would be streaming down my face at the thought of leaving her, and always I longed for the time when I could return home and we could be together again. The first thing I would do when I got back from school was rush to the field and call Folly. She would always throw up her head, give a great whinny of welcome and canter over at full tilt to greet me. We loved each other.

Folly was a continual source of amazement and amusement as we continued our show-ring education together. I remember that at one small local agricultural show, when we had been ignominiously left 'down the line', she showed her disapproval by lashing out at one of the cars parked at the ringside, and dealing most effectively with the glass of a headlamp. The car turned out to belong to the judge! A week or so later, her pride was suitably restored by the award of a 'Reserve Champion' rosette, a most unexpected glory, and received quite by accident. The winners of each of the pony classes were eligible, and the two bigger ponies, both ridden by the same rider, were certainties for the awards. However, in the circumstances, they could not appear simultaneously for the Championship, so Folly and I, *faute de mieux*, became the runners-up.

By this time, she had earned a reputation for her prowess in gymkhana events. She loved bending races, potato races, musical chairs and the rest, and knew all the answers. I loved it when I was cheered on by the locals who would often come up to the show ground after work to watch the antics of the young riders. There was a marvellous loud-speaker van man, Mr Milton, who attended most of the shows in this capacity and knew all of the riders' names. He played the music from his gramophone in the van for Musical Chairs in which we rode around the outside of the circle to the music and when it stopped, we riders had to jump off and make a dash on foot to the chairs with the ponies in tow. You can imagine the chaos as ponies got mixed up when riders threw themselves at a chair, and Mr Milton would accompany this uproar with a hilarious commentary.

In a misguided moment I decided to teach Folly to bow, at which she became most adept, and she thoroughly delighted in the procedure. She had two versions – one the debutante's with a foreleg thrust gracefully forward beneath bowed head, and the other the Muslim's, head prostrated over both bent knees. But I began to regret having taught her, for while I was busy gathering an elusive potato, or turning my coat inside out, she would go into her act, to the delight of the crowd, so that I, when ready to remount would discover her prostrate. She learnt all sorts of tricks; she would stand on a box, play hide-and-seek, kiss me, and if she got half a chance, come into the kitchen. No pony could ever have given a child more pleasure.

When I grew too big to ride her, I decided to try her in harness, and we bought a little governess cart, painted primrose yellow and black – extremely smart. Some days she would behave perfectly and some days she wouldn't! So, anyone coming for a drive did so at risk of life and limb. She became used to all sorts of loads. We'd go and cut grass, and sit on top of the pile, but likely as not would be tossed off, arms and legs flying in all directions before we got back to the stable yard. But she did once go well enough to win a third prize in a driving class at the local gymkhana, and I remember John standing at her head most professionally in the 'Haydon' manner.

Over the years we would 'lend her out' to other children. She would wait for an opportunity to slip away unnoticed and come home, always demolishing prize vegetables on the way. I remember one

time in particular, when Chips had already come to Lytham. Folly was then with a small boy about four miles from us, and lived in a large field with every luxury. But she was not satisfied, and showed her disapproval by escaping at the dead of night. She returned unerringly, along roads and over the level crossing – frightening the signalman in the process – to the field in which she had lived until I grew too big to ride her any longer.

Unfortunately, the gate was shut, so she wandered around and eventually found an interesting entrance which she thought worth investigating. In she went, and began to feast joyfully on all manner of expensive plants, until, thoroughly gorged, she withdrew gracefully, and was later put in one of the fields by a local who recognised her as mine. In the afternoon I happened to cycle by, and was astonished to see her placidly watching me over the fence. I caught her, and was preparing to cycle over to Wrea Green to return the truant, when an irate gentleman stormed up, demanding an explanation of the overnight disappearance of his life's work. I regret to say that when I realised what had happened, I burst into laughter, and we took our leave in the knowledge that at least one person did not appreciate the qualities of my first love.

Sheila riding Folly at their first horse show.

Folly in the governess cart.

With John, Patch, a friend and her dog.

Chapter Two – Ponies Galore

During my schooldays I had various ponies of one size, shape or another. Folly was soon joined by a chestnut mare called Sweet Sue, whom we bought to show in the 13.2 h.h. classes; but within a few months she had grown out of the class, and had to compete with bigger ponies in the 14.2 h.h. She was no 'tip-topper', as we soon realised, but I gained experience on her and soon tried to teach her to jump. However, Sue was very reluctant to leave the ground at all, and though she did become fairly proficient within a certain limit, she never looked as if she enjoyed it. Indeed, when she was airborne, she jumped in such a pained manner that we were always reminded of a swan in distress. She never came near to taking Folly's place in my heart, for Folly was a real character and the sort of pony one could not help loving. Sue was just another pony, but Folly seemed almost human, and was my best friend for years.

Perhaps the best pony I had was a 13.2 h.h. Welsh-Arab gelding called Sherif. He was a beautiful pony, having inherited all the best Arab traits as well as the hardiness and common sense of the Welsh breed. He was the most superb jumper, and his style was impeccable. Imagine a little grey pony with flying mane and outstretched Araby tail taking each fence in his stride, with never a change of pace, and the picture will give you an idea of how Sherry was. I had enormous fun on him, and great success too. He was good-looking enough to do well in local showing classes and was superb at gymkhana events, his forte being the 'Walk, Trot and Gallop' race - for he had a terrific turn of speed and could hold his own with far bigger ponies. I was always fascinated by his little curved ears, a legacy from his Arab forbears, and whenever they were forward he looked as sweet a pony as one could ever wish to see. Sometimes, though, he laid them flat back against his head, and put on a real scowl, his muzzle and eyes screwed up and wrinkled with temper and annoyance.

We had no local Pony Club in the district, and no hunting, so I didn't have the type of pony club lifestyle described in the Pullein-Thompson sisters' novels. My parents did organise entertainments for the children who had, or could hire, ponies in the Christmas and Easter holidays. We had gymkhanas, obstacle rides and treasure hunts. I remember particularly a brilliant treasure hunt when we started with a stirrup cup of Bovril at the local hotel, and made for the first clue in Lytham Hall Park. All the clues were in rhyme, and took us four or five miles to a neighbouring village, where an obliging farmer stabled our mounts in a barn while we had a picnic lunch in the village school. After lunch we resumed the chase, riding in a circle back to the hotel. The clues led us to a ghost in a dove-cote, a raft on the pond on a village green, a scarecrow with pockets stuffed with things which had to be brought back and many other exciting difficulties ending with:

> 'A fearsome dragon in its lair,
>
> Watching o'er the treasure rare.'

This was a benign Patch in a shed in a field. These adventures on horseback were followed by a Christmas party, or – if later in the year – a picnic in the field.

My parents were wonderfully supportive about everything to do with my riding of the ponies until the end of my sixteenth year when, in equestrian terms, I became an adult. From the time I was twelve years old Daddy had thrown himself into the show scene with the greatest enthusiasm although he did say that he got bossed around by me more than anyone else in all his life. Mummy, on the other hand, was more circumspect. She did not take to the show jumpers and was terrified that in time I would fall for one of the men and spoil all her dreams. She need not have worried. I was far too involved with the ponies, and too busy for it even to occur to me to look in the direction of a boy with any romantic interest.

Sherif and I went to the Richmond Royal Show, where we were third, the two winners both jumped five feet one inch and divided first place. We were 'out' at four feet ten inches, not through hitting a fence – this he rarely did – but by refusing a gate before sailing over perfectly the next time. That same year, my last in the 13.2 h.h. classes, he won the Southport Jumping Championship. In fact, he was placed every time out.

We used to go to most of the shows in the vicinity during the holidays, and usually my mother and father came along to provide the necessary moral and practical support. One particular morning, we were off to a show but my mother had a dreadful cold and decided to stay at home. In our absence she intended, for once, to take the opportunity of going to bed, so that she could be 'proper poorly' all day long. The ponies were led into the horsebox, and with my father driving, Marjorie the groom beside him, and John, myself and a girl-friend in the back, we set out for the showground.

This show had a Horticultural Section, and after the conclusion of my classes, John, Jean and I wandered into the tent, where I knew an auction of all the prize produce was to take place later on. With Mother's condition in mind, I had determined to look out for something suitable in the way of flowers or fruit to take back to the invalid. We soon saw a plateful of luscious black grapes and decided that this was just the thing. It remained only for us to bid for the fruit.

The marquee grew more and more crowded, and at last the sale began. We kept our eyes fixed on the grapes, and eventually saw the auctioneer's assistant put them up to his stand. They must be the next lot, we thought, so I was pushed up on to a table top from where I could be seen when the bidding took place. I was really quite terrified at the prospect of my task, but as the opening bids were called, I plucked up a little courage, and soon, to the vast amusement of the crowd, the bidding resolved itself into a battle between a man and myself. I was determined to have those grapes, and as the man raised his price, so I countered him with another sixpenny increase, until at just under a pound, he retired defeated, leaving me to approach the Auctioneer's platform to receive my prize. I nearly collapsed when the clerk, instead of passing over the expected grapes, proudly presented me with a miniature Japanese garden made of small shells and stones. My face fell a mile, and everyone in the tent heard my dismayed, "But I was bidding for the grapes!" They were the NEXT lot, but the crowd was so amused that by public demand the hideous garden was exchanged for grapes, and we went home, proudly bearing our prize to my mother.

My brother John, who had a wonderful seat as a child, only rode under protest and on the strictest understanding that once he was on the ground again, he could forget all about the pony and its needs. But he was always ready for Cowboys and Indians in the sand dunes. He and I, on Sherif and Folly, would leap from mound to mound, to the consternation, in the summer of bathers modestly disrobing out of sight of the beach, and of courting couples who became so immobile from fright that they were probably saved many a nasty mix-up. We must have been very unpopular!

We did our schooling over jumps in the field, at the end of a cart track flanked by a tidal dyke. At low tide in hot weather the water that remained was anything but salubrious, and barely covered the bottles, jars, tins and other jetsam always to be found on the beds of such streams. I must explain that the path to the fields formed a right-angled unfenced bridge over the dyke, so that one could, in the dark, or if unwary, come through the gate and fall straight into the water. One day, after John, Marjorie and I had been jumping the ponies, we joined my mother at the gate. It was a hot day and she was wearing a fresh white-and-green cotton frock and white sandals. She opened the gate for us and mounted her bicycle, then suddenly remembered something she wanted to say to us. Unfortunately, as she turned her head, she forgot to turn her handle-bars too, and suddenly there was no sign of her – only a bike going in one direction and two legs disappearing into the dyke on the other.

You can imagine the ensuing 'flap'. My brother yelling that she was drowned, Marjorie gathering scattering ponies, and I climbing over the gate screaming that I was coming. I peered over the edge, and there she was, covered in slimy mud, her sandals floating downstream like two miniature swans. She had miraculously missed all the sharp edges, which might have seriously hurt her, and it only needed my father's roar of laughter, when he arrived a minute later, to change drama into comedy. How we laughed – Mother too. She had to ride back home almost naked, as her filthy frock would have ruined the car seats, and she smelled horrible.

When I grew out of the 13.2 h.h. class, I had two 14.2 h.h. ponies, Ecstasy, a show-pony on which I had considerable success in the north, and Beau Brummel, whom I bought from Margaret Hough. Brummell was a wonderful pony, more like a 'little horse', a beautiful mover and a fine jumper. He would have made me a grand hunter had there been any hunting, and a splendid one-day event pony if there had been any Pony Club here in those days. When I was looking for an eventing horse, his was the picture I carried in my mind. But he was a cross-patch in the stable. To clip him was a nightmare, and he loathed a vet. Once he swallowed the thermometer, and it was never found. On another occasion he nipped my father, who, quick as lightning picked up his full water bucket, and threw the contents over him. He never so much as pulled a face at him after that. I made great strides in the show-ring on him, entering showing, jumping and gymkhana classes, and he was grand at Hunter Trials.

For some time, we had had a local girl to look after the ponies who, but for 'a bit of a gland', as she used to say would have been condemned to life in an office. Marjorie Whitehurst was her name, affectionately known to us as Margarine. She had had no professional training, but had picked up what she could from the riding stable, where she had worked, and had added to it as much as she could learn from books. She was great fun. Many a time she and I and John had nearly rolled out of our saddles with laughter, her mimicry and priceless turn of speech were a joy to us all. She was extremely conscientious, and taught me the habit of doing everything in the stable methodically and thoroughly. No start was too early for her, and she never grizzled, however late we got home after a show. No two children ever had a better mentor – forthright, honest, and high-principled. My mother saw to it that as soon as we were old enough, we realised and appreciated her worth.

My father decided that the ponies should get used to dogs, both in and out of the stable. Accordingly, one Christmas he came home with the sweetest of puppies as a present for John. He was a cross between a Welsh and Cumberland sheepdog, with a black patch over one eye. He was so fat that he waddled when he walked, with his tummy nearly touching the floor after a meal. We were delighted with him, and soon he was quite at home in the stable with Folly and Sherif.

We were still deciding on a name when Marjorie told us that he was being called Carlo by a frequent visitor to the stable. This so horrified us that he became the obvious Patch without more ado. Unfortunately, being a winter baby and spending as much time on the cold floor as in his warm box, he developed rickets. We fed him raw eggs, lime water and gallons of milk and his legs were bathed in seawater twice a day. This treatment completely cured him and he was able to get into mischief like any other puppy.

When he was big enough, he went everywhere with the ponies. He had a marvellous temperament and never showed any resentment at the rough treatment he regularly received when we played with him. We taught him to jump all sorts of obstacles, to lie down and die, to play hide-and-seek, to beg, and to 'sing a song' (this last a direct challenge to my father, who is tone-deaf). He became adept at hunt the slipper, and was a continual source of joy to young visitors. If we were going to play football, Patch would be dressed in an old striped jersey with his forelegs through the sleeves, his hind-legs in a pair of my gym-knickers with a hole cut in the crutch for his tail.

All his life he adored balloons, which for some obscure reason he connected with the words 'ninety-nine'. Sometimes, by way of Christmas decoration we had them on the ceiling, and if he came into the house, he would sit for hours mesmerised by the sight. He got us into lots of scrapes too.

I remember one day, when he was following Marjorie to the house, he stopped to investigate a friendly smelling street-lamp. Suddenly he realised that he had been left behind, and tore around the corner slap-bang into a very small man carrying a very large sheet of glass. Down sprawled the man, and up went the glass before crashing into a thousand pieces on the pavement. Patch went yelping after Marjorie, as if he were the one who had been hurt. Fortunately, there were no injuries, only a slightly cut thumb, but Daddy wasn't very pleased when the damage claim came in.

Neither was he exactly delighted when one evening a man came to the back door with a pair of well-bitten trousers. By this time the ponies were stabled in beautiful roomy boxes behind Lytham Hall, then occupied by one of the Ministries – the stables were a mile or so distant from the house, so every day we had to cycle there to ride. John and I were coming home with Patch through the park after riding when we saw what we thought was a trespasser on a bicycle. Without a thought, we shouted, "Seize him!" and Patch did, with unfortunate results both to the innocent victim, and to my brother and myself when my father got around to dealing with us.

Patch used to go with the horsebox to all the shows and had an uncanny habit of finding the nearest way to the refreshment tent. Here he would sit at the feet of anyone who happened to be eating a meat pie, and would look up in an anguished way, with his tongue lolling out. Like most dogs he hated cats, except his own stable mates. One Sunday morning he came, as he often did, to meet us from church, and on the way home spotted a lovely specimen of a ginger cat. Quick as lightning the chase was on and I shall never see a better cavaletti executed at the gallop. There was a long row of fishermen's cottages whose front gardens were separated by yard-high brick walls, and over these, one after the other, with no variation of speed, come what may, went pursued and pursuer. It really was a poem of movement, but as cats will, this unsportsmanlike specimen took evasive action, and at the end of the line of buildings, she climbed a tree leaving a panting Patch frustrated at its base. We hurriedly collected him and made off before any irate gardeners became aware of our private tornado.

When we went to the Hall stables he had a lovely time – in the fields with the ponies, and chasing rabbits and hares with much noise but little success. He used to like going up into the loft, with its round unglassed windows where he could sun himself and watch the comings and goings below. Mother was glad when he took up residence there permanently, as she had had enough of the dirt and his hairs left all over everything. She used to say we had Patch's hairs fried, poached, boiled, grilled and roasted.

By the time Marjorie, Patch, and the successors to my first ponies had arrived on the scene, my father had become the 'horsiest of the horsey', and Mother viewed with alarm the upheaval which was taking place in the domestic sphere. Being a business man, he took a poor view of any activity which paid no dividends. He therefore decided the thing to do was to breed top-class show-ponies and to use the big southern shows as shop-windows. What he completely left out of his calculations was the fact that he'd have nothing to show for five years, and by that time I'd be out of the Juvenile classes. He bought a stallion, the Arab Rizaab, and a couple of Thoroughbred mares, to the delight of Marjorie and me, and the consternation of my mother. He went to see the Trustees of the Clifton estate, and arranged to take over the lovely old yard and an eighty-acre pasture. So, Folly, Sherif and Beau Brummell joined the breeding stock in the stables where generations of Cliftons had kept their famous racehorses.

Rizaab had been well schooled by his previous owner (what a dressage horse he would have made for me!), and my father decided that a few successes in the show-ring might help with outside services. He persuaded Lieutenant Colonel Jack Hance to come up and have a look at him. The outcome was a preliminary week's tuition for Rizaab and Marjorie. That was how I came to possess the rudiments of schooling a horse, for when the term ended, I made Marjorie show me everything she had learned, and afterwards I practised it on my ponies. With a broad grin she would say to me, "Now! A little equitittle by Marjorie Whittle."

The next time Colonel Hance came up I was home on holiday, so I listened to everything he said and later carried it out on the ponies. As a result, Sherif and Beau Brummell won many more awards in show classes than their conformation warranted. I'm sure Colonel Hance would have been the first to agree that small children and their ponies didn't excite him in the least, but I did unwittingly on one occasion make him aware of my presence. The household was gathering for lunch, and as I walked through the kitchen, I asked what we were going to eat. "Plaice," said my mother, whereupon I remarked wistfully, "There's turbot at the fishmonger's." This brought no response beyond a casual, "Is there?" Undeflated, I went to my desk in the nursery, took stock of my financial resources and decided to buy my own lunch. You can imagine the reactions around the table when, after the family dish had arrived, a large, luscious-looking fillet of turbot was placed before me – my own paid-out-of-my-pocket-money choice. This made an impact even on the imperturbable Colonel, who remarked that he knew children blew their money on such atrocities as ice-cream, but never before had he come across one willing and able to indulge a taste for luxury foods. And I'm afraid this was something I still did whenever opportunity offered. In fact, my mother accused me of living from meal to meal.

The months went by and the first foals were on the way. The job had become too big for Marjorie and we had to have a stud-manager, so my father engaged an ex-Weedon officer, Colonel Hodgson. He walked around the yard a lot in highly polished brown boots, tapping the sides of them with his whip. I do not remember seeing him doing much hands-on work, but he was certainly decorative, enthusiastic and kind. In what little time he had to spare in school holidays during the next year, he taught John and me a lot.

My mother, as the weeks went by, began to have visions of us becoming quite poverty-stricken unless something happened to curb my father's enthusiasm. Being a wise woman, she didn't fight the issue, but rather on the lines of 'if one works in a chocolate factory one can't eat the stuff,' she encouraged the buying of more stock until we were cluttered up with twenty-three animals of various shapes and sizes. Feed and staff bills became enormous, and, following one or two accidents, caused my father to halt in his stride. Even the heated mushroom beds he'd made, at terrific outlay, refused to become a paying proposition until he handed them over on a most unbusinesslike basis to a local nurseryman – after which they rioted almost overnight!

The last straw was when our biggest pasture was wanted for the Home Farm and my father decided to sell out. We sold Rizaab and one or two mares and foals, which had won awards at the Arab Show at Roehampton, and the rest went to the Leicester sales, to go at almost give-away prices. The second stallion, Algayam, the delight of Marjorie's heart, was sold, after being withdrawn from the sale, to Mrs Edlin of Thurnby, who had him at stud for many years and always gave any of us who called a tremendous welcome.

. Sherif jumping a double bar in the field

Chapter Three – Blithe Spirit

When I was sixteen and in my last term at Haunton Hall I took eight School Certificate Examinations and passed them all with very high marks. After the summer exams pupils were expected to stay on for three more weeks, but Daddy had explained to Sister Patrice three or four years earlier that I was needed at home to show the ponies and, to my joy, she had agreed as my school work was very good. This pattern had been set since then, and the day after the last examination every summer, I would be collected and removed by Daddy as quietly as possible, to the great envy of the rest of the girls.

Mummy had been extremely keen for me to stay on at school for another year to take the higher exams, but I had been so forceful in stating that I was going to continue somehow with the horses and I agreed to her caveat that I would not set out to be a show jumper and I would suffer a course of shorthand and typing at Blackpool so that I had something to fall back on. My parents were quite adamant that I should not join the ranks of the show jumpers, for they considered that the time had come for me to assume a more lady-like demeanour. It was decided, then, that a show hack, that mannequin of the horse world, should be found for me. After a number of wild-goose chases we eventually, quite by accident, found ourselves at a farm in Yorkshire. We had lost our way and somehow turned into this yard by mistake. There we were shown a five-year-old brown gelding, which had been used by his late owner for carrying grain to cattle in the fields.

My parents were frankly horrified when I insisted that he was the one, but I had looked at him very carefully, trying to visualise what he would be like if he were fatter and in good condition. He had a sweet little head, plenty of 'rein' and a short back. He moved with a low swinging stride and showed promise of extravagant action combined with the 'look' of the true hack type. My parents decided to follow my intuition, and the horse was bought. Arrangements were made for him to travel to Lytham the following week, and in due course my father drove over to Yorkshire again. Imagine my father's face when he was told on arrival that our purchase had met with a slight accident out in the field, and had got rather a nasty cut between the front legs. He was all for leaving the horse behind, but eventually was convinced all would be well in time, and our Lytham stables soon had a new tenant.

Marjorie was still with us when he first arrived, so together we spent days, weeks and months on this horse. He was given all sorts of fattening foods, such as boiled potatoes and even rice, but very few oats as we discovered these only made him feel too full of himself. Gradually I taught him to walk, trot and canter smoothly whenever he was asked, to do a 'figure of eight' at the canter, to rein back and 'half-pass' to either side, all of which would be required of him in his show-ring career.

I taught him to back, first of all, by standing him against a fence, while not 'giving' with my hands, I gave him a gentle squeeze with my legs. Until then he had understood this to mean that he should move forward, but now he found himself face to face with a fence. He did the natural thing, and stepped back. I made a fuss of him, and repeated the performance. He realised what I wanted, and we were able to go away from the railings and rein back in the open spaces. The fence again came in useful when I began to teach him the half-pass, to begin with I halted him at right-angles to the fence and with his head right up against it. I made him go sideways in an extremely ragged full-pass by guiding his forehand to either side with one rein or the other, and using the diagonal leg to control his hindquarters. Again, it was not long before he learnt the lesson, and once he could produce a full-pass, it was a relatively simple matter to half-pass.

Soon he began to put on weight, and to blossom before our eyes. It became apparent that here was a horse! Great plans for the next season were laid. A name had to be chosen, something truly representative of all his grace, exuberance and aristocratic bearing. Blithe Spirit came to mind and I decided to enter him in a few of the local shows, to give him a little ring experience before his southern debut at the start of the following season. At one of these shows we met that great showman, Sam Marsh, a very well-known hack exhibitor. He consented to come up to Lytham for a while and help me in training Blithe Spirit. Sam Marsh had had a lifetime of experience in the show-ring, so his advice was invaluable, and together we worked daily in the field, transforming a young green horse into a lovely, well-mannered animal.

To Richmond, we went, and had almost won the class, even to the point of photographers making appointments to meet us afterwards outside the ring. But the strain of keeping up a façade of gentlemanly behaviour must have been too much for Blithe Spirit, for in the final walk-round, he went completely haywire and misbehaved, not once, but twice, right in front of the judges. Such a display of ill-manners simply could not be overlooked, so down the line we went, and all the dreams of a beautiful blue Richmond rosette were gone. Naturally, I was most disappointed, but there was no sense in brooding over a misfortune, so I decided that the next time I must make sure that obedience was second nature to him. I looked on this experience as a warning of what can happen to spoil everything when it seems as if nothing can take away victory, and, bitter though the lesson had been, it served to impress on me that, like a child, a horse needs a firm hand, and needs no encouragement to take advantage of someone not prepared to instil discipline. Above all, I learnt the importance of being a good sportsperson. It is easy enough to wear the victor's laurels, but how much more difficult to smile in the face of defeat, especially after tasting the sweetness of victory.

But at the International Show in July we had our revenge, and how sweet it was! A week beforehand, having decided that perhaps an expert's schooling would control high spirits, I telephoned Count Orssich and to my amazement he knew immediately who I was. He suggested that Blithe Spirit and I go to his farm for a week's training during the week prior to White City and travel directly from there up to London and the Royal International.

Every day, Blithe Spirit and I went into the indoor school and worked there under the guidance of the Count. He made me realise the importance of smooth paces and transitions up and down through walk, trot and canter. I have never forgotten how he described the execution of the transitions for which we were striving. He likened the horse to a car, and its paces to the gears; the driver changes gear, either smoothly or otherwise, according to his ability, and it is exactly the same with the rider and his horse. Good horsemen and good drivers have much in common, for they will both produce a picture of smoothness, precision, and above all, of ease. For ease is the predominant impression given when anything is being done really well.

I was also taught how to lunge a horse correctly, in cavesson and side reins, and to make it really work and not just run around on the end of a rein. I was taught to recognise the moment when the animal goes with the correct flexion, and to keep it there for longer and longer until it becomes natural to it. All this was of tremendous help to me when I returned home with Blithe Spirit, for he was always liable to become excited at a show and to offset this had to be given an enormous amount of work on the preceding day. Rather than wear myself out as well on these occasions, I would resort to the use of the lunge-rein, and would stand watching him work for the two hours.

At Winkfield Farm, the intervening days which separated us from the Hack class at White City melted away, and soon we were traveling to the Stadium in the horsebox. As usual, it was early in the morning. Only the very knowledgeable people were gathered about the ringside as we walked, trotted and cantered round on the green turf of that awe-inspiring place. The judges began to call us in, and I was brought in at the head of the line. Sam Marsh, however – always the showman – sidled in above us, and for his pains earned the doubtful distinction of giving the first individual show. It was a good one, and in the stand my parents despaired of our being able to equal such a performance. But Blithe Spirit, was determined to behave perfectly, and came out to give the show of his life. He went like a dream and I had high hopes. The preliminary judging came to a close, and out we all filed, wondering just in what order we would find ourselves in the final line-up that afternoon.

In due course we all rode into the ring again, to give the crowd a chance to see all the entries, and to decide on their own personal choice, in comparison with the judges' placings. Blithe Spirit and I were called into the first place, and how proud I felt standing out in front of the line, among the flower-beds! Photographers were on all sides, flashing away with their cameras, and then there was the thrill of seeing the White City 'first' rosette clipped on to Blithe Spirit's bridle. We cantered elegantly round the ring before returning to the horsebox. There I left my horse, and walked in a daze back to the stand, and to my parents.

How pleased, too, was Count Orssich. But he warned me not to be disappointed if we didn't win the Championship in the evening. This is open to the first and second prize-winners in each of the three Hack classes, and takes place under floodlights late in the evening performance. I wondered how Blithe Spirit would react to the dazzling lights. We passed through the tunnel which leads to the Collecting Ring inside the Stadium. 'What on earth can this be?' was clearly the question he was asking as he gazed fascinated at the bright arena, with its spotlights playing on the beautiful horses of the famous Spanish Quadrille. The sound of applause, too, seemed to be magnified a thousand times, and I really began to think that this was another occasion on which manners would go by the board. But not at all. The Quadrille was over, it remained for us to go through the usual routine and Blithe Spirit went like an old hand, and took not the slightest notice of the band as we passed and repassed their stand while they played on merrily.

Again, we were called in first – the Championship was ours, and another most exciting moment. The Duchess of Kent presented me with the trophy, and talked for a minute or so before returning to the Royal Box. As we cantered round, the floodlights were dimmed, and to the applause of the gigantic crowd, the Champion Hack for 1954 was picked out in spotlights.

It was something never to be forgotten, for this is an award greatly coveted in Hack circles. As one exhibitor remarked afterwards, she had been trying to gain the honour for years and years, yet here was I, only seventeen, fortunate enough to be the victor at my first attempt.

The months ahead were filled with shows as usual, and I was looking forward to competing with Blithe Spirit for the title of Show Hack of the Year at Harringay late in October. In the meantime, however, we met some visitors from Venezuela, and soon, due to our mutual interest in horses, they were frequent visitors at our home. When they were due to sail back to the Americas, they invited me to accompany them for a few months. It was too good an opportunity to miss, and arrangements were made for my passage on the French liner, Antilles. There was one drawback, though, for by this time we had no one at all to look after Blithe Spirit and he could not be left in cold storage until my return. We decided he would have to be sold, and before long we were taking him to his new home with Mrs Mackintosh at Holyport. She was a prominent competitor in the show hack world.

I was sad to see him go, but it had to be, and secretly I was longing to find another horse to take his place as soon as I came back from my travels. At this point, I may add, that both my parents hoped that, after seeing a bit of the world, I would give up all thoughts of a life connected with horses. How wrong they were!

Blithe Spirit winning the Hack class at White City, 1953.

Chapter Four – A Partnership Begins

It was December when I returned from South America, flying home from Caracas in one of the giant stratocruisers. We had had engine trouble over Bermuda, and been grounded there for twenty-four hours. Then London Airport was fog-bound, so the plane was diverted to Prestwick. My parents had been waiting for me in London, and it was not until six in the morning that we were reunited after my three-month trip.

I was now nearly eighteen, and as my mother so often stressed, should have been well on the road to a successful career. But the question was – along which path should I set out? I had no particular urge to follow any orthodox professions, and had already attempted an architectural course, which had resulted in dismal failure. The matter was brought up time and time again until I was almost in despair. I still had no idea of what I should like to do, and eventually I agreed to undergo a secretarial course while making up my mind. I duly learnt the intricacies of shorthand and became proficient with a typewriter and the display of these accomplishments appeased my mother, especially when I was able to help my father with his masses of correspondence.

My stay abroad had done nothing to quench my longings for another horse, and though I broached the subject at my peril, both parents were absolutely against the idea. But it was something I could not help talking about, and I began a campaign to break down their resistance.

I still had the money from the sale of Blithe Spirit, but in all other ways I was dependent upon my parents. If I bought a horse, they might throw me out and I would have no home and nowhere to keep him, but ignoring the danger of pursuing my cause, I kept on and on about buying another horse to the extent that it provoked the most almighty blow-up with my mother. I was adamant that I was going to have some sort of career with horses, and she was equally determined that I should not. I told her that I had hated the shorthand and typing course that she had made me take. It ended with me in floods of tears, rushing upstairs to my bedroom and locking the door. I believed that this was the end, that my mother was totally irreconcilable and that I would never be allowed to find another horse as a successor to Blithe

Spirit. Daddy returned home to find both of us still very upset, and the outcome was that by morning the ban was lifted.

I imagine that they had had a bad night coming to this conclusion, and that Daddy must have said, 'Well, we do know she is very good with horses, and look at the money she has made already!' Looking back this set the pattern for my life, my unalterable will to ride and compete, and my determination to make a living out of horses.

The hope of finding another hack capable of equalling Blithe Spirit was extremely remote. Show jumping, too, was out of the question, as my parents would never change their minds. My mother was totally opposed to the idea of her daughter joining the ranks of those she clearly thought to be a threat to my virginity. I did not want to upset her any farther. I had therefore to decide what field of equestrian sport I should enter.

Although I had never been to a horse trial, I felt most attracted to a competition demanding talent in three distinct directions. My experience with the ponies and show hacks would stand me in good stead as far as the dressage and show jumping phases were concerned, and I hoped that my ability to ride across country was something which could be developed. Whatever I did, I was not interested just to take part. I wanted to win, to be the best.

Having decided, therefore, that this was my goal, the only thing I lacked was a horse. I scanned the columns of *Horse and Hound.* Up and down the country I went in answer to the most promising advertisements, but none of the animals I saw conformed to the picture I carried in my mind's eye – which was a larger edition of Beau Brummel, the pony I had had when still in juvenile classes. I hadn't in any case expected to find a suitable horse straightaway.

The talents required for a trials animal are diverse in the extreme; while it is a comparatively simple job to discover one that can jump, or is good-looking and a good mover - to find a horse which combines all these virtues is almost an impossibility. A good jumper will quite often prove incapable of settling down to the work of the dressage horse, and similarly an animal with ability to make a name for himself in the dressage phase will be lacking in boldness or courage when it comes to the jumping and cross-country. The perfect horse for trials must possess, first and foremost the right temperament. He must be capable of displaying calm in the dressage arena, and equable enough to give his attention to the rider's demands in strange surroundings. Then he must also be high-spirited and bold enough to go across country, over terrifying obstacles, and be clever in his jumping to get himself and rider out of trouble in an emergency. He must be fast enough to record bonus points, and possess strength and stamina for the tiring speed and endurance of a three-day trial. On top of all this, he must be able to adjust himself from jumping at speed over fixed fences to the precision jumping of the third phase in the show jumping. With all these points to bear in mind, no wonder it took me a long time to find a horse in which I could be interested.

My search went on for a couple of months. In desperation I put an advertisement in the 'Horses Wanted' column, and was soon swamped with offers. These I carefully eliminated one by one, until even that large pile had dwindled to nil, and I was still horseless. Then came a belated reply, and with it a photograph of the animal concerned and the offer of a week's trial. The horse's name was Sanction, and he was owned by a lady in Sussex who had bred him while she was still living in Ireland. Mrs Lake had sold him as a three-year-old; but when she had subsequently seen how well he performed in the hunting field, she bought him back, and had continued to hunt him herself with the Meath until she came over to live in England. Sanction came to England too, but she had little time to look after him, and he became more of a liability than an asset to his owner. So, when my advertisement appeared, Mrs Lake decided to write and offer me her horse.

At last I had been really attracted by a reply. Arrangements were made for this seven-year-old dun gelding to travel north from his home in Sussex. I could scarcely contain my impatience for his arrival at the station, and when he finally walked out of the train, I took an immediate liking to him. Again, I half-closed my eyes, and tried to see him as he would look in time. He was alert, and showed plenty of interest in what was going on around him, and although he was by no means beautiful, he had that undefinable air always to be found in a good horse. On top of all this, he had a dark eel stripe running down his back and 'donkey' markings on his front legs, points which old and sage horsemen maintain are the hallmark of a good 'un. His rather odd dun colour, the black mark along his spine and the lines on his front legs could all be traced as a legacy from his Highland pony grand-dam, for though his sire was Thoroughbred, his dam was half-Arab and half-Highland. The mixture of breeds did not worry me in the slightest, for personally I believe a splash of common blood does no horse any harm, and will perhaps add the calm temperament and sound sense that is often to be found lacking in the majority of Thoroughbred animals. But this horse was perhaps an exceptional example of such mixed breeding, for he seemed to have taken the best from each strain. He had a full sister, but she never grew to be more than fifteen hands – otherwise I might even have tried to buy her as well.

During his week's trial I rode him often, and still nothing happened to change the opinion I now held – that this was my horse. The deal was made, and Mrs Lake lost a horse that was to gain so many thrills and successes for me. I didn't like the name Sanction at all, so after family conferences we found that the most popular proposal was High and Mighty. But as this was too long for everyday use, we nicknamed him Chips.

Unfortunately, the long train journey in cold weather resulted in him developing the most dreadful cough and cold, and I began to wonder whether I should actually have him for very much longer. He was dosed morning, noon, and night, and his poor condition worried me very much. Eventually he began to improve, and slowly returned to health. Now I could start to train him properly and find out just how well he could jump, since – on account of his lack of condition – I had previously been unable to do this. Until this time all Chips' jumping had been done in the company of others out hunting, but regardless of how well an animal may jump in those circumstances it doesn't follow he will be as willing when asked to perform alone, in 'cold blood'. All I knew was that the ability to jump was in him, so my problem was to bring it out for individual performance.

There was no point in trying to jump at once, for Chips knew nothing more than an ordinary hunter or private horse which knows how to give his owner a pleasant ride. I was not going to give him a chance to gain the upper hand at the start of our partnership, which might very easily have happened if I hadn't controlled my impatience. Accordingly, I began his training with this aim of obedience in mind. We focused on learning to walk, trot and canter correctly, with smooth transitions. He was by nature well-balanced and moved freely and straight, so I had not much difficulty with these preliminaries.

Then he had to learn to rein back calmly, and with measured tread, and to stand immobile when asked. Funnily enough, he found these halts one of the most difficult things of all, for I insisted that each time he stopped he should come to rest with all four legs 'square'. Without fail I would find he was trailing one hind-leg, and my efforts to put this right by urging him to take a half step forward resulted in his crossing legs and doing everything short of turning himself inside out. At last he did suddenly realise what he had to do, and would then very deliberately bring up the trailing leg to join the others, moving it into line with a stamp of distrust at such a triviality. Please note that I never tried to make him step back to be square, one should always ask the horse to move forward into a square halt.

I began to try him over small obstacles, both in the field and over anything easily negotiable which we found on our ordinary road exercise, and I realised as we progressed that his jumping left much to be desired. He was very 'spooky' and imagined he could see all kinds of terrifying objects lurking behind the jumps. It was a problem to get him to overcome this habit, and to make him go over without peering round suspiciously. I always let him have a look at the fence before asking him to jump, so he had no real excuse for misbehaviour, but even so he would still produce these fits of spooking from time to time. Even when we rode along the roads, I had to be wary of a sudden swerve into the path of the traffic. When we passed parked cars, he seemed to expect a door to be opened in his face. When a particularly big truck or bus came towards us he would whirl around on the slippery tarmac, frightening me nearly to death.

I had bought Chips late in February, and by the middle of April he had progressed sufficiently for me to consider him ready to compete in the local hunter trials. We had no hunt but teams of four and pairs as well as individuals. Several of the riders had been with me in the same pony jumping classes as juveniles and one or two of them were older than me, and already doing well in adult classes. I found someone to make up a pair and was invited to join three others to complete a four. Chips jumped with great gusto in the company of others in the classes for pairs and teams. But in the Individual competition he wanted nothing to do with jumping. He refused adamantly, he did not even want to canter towards the first fence. His behaviour caused many of the members to raise eyebrows at one another, and to whisper that, "Sheila must have left her eye for a horse on the other side of the Atlantic." In their opinion, my hope of producing this horse for future competition in horse trials proper was ludicrous, but I wasn't going to take any notice of what others thought of Chips.

We were going to wait until everyone had gone home and then we would jump the course. Mummy and Daddy had come to watch our first competition and could not believe how badly Chips had let us down. Daddy was all in favour of staying on to help sort him out, but Mummy went white at the prospect and said she would stay in the car.

Battle commenced as soon as Chips refused again at the first fence, and I hit him with my short whip just behind my leg on both sides. so he would think he was encased and could not run off sideways. This may seem cruel to those of you who hate punishment, but I was giving Chips not only my love, but a good life with every equine comfort, and my financial circumstances could not stand him being useless through a ridiculous and unnecessary quirk of his nature. When John and I were young, we were expected to behave and do as we were told. If we deliberately refused to follow the rules, we were punished, and when the transgression went further, we were slapped, which might have stung for a few seconds, but did us no harm at all and effectively stopped us in our tracks.

Now with Chips this was a near parallel situation and he also had to choose whether he would continue to refuse to jump without equine friends around him, or realise he was facing a battle he was not going to win. Eventually I prevailed, and he jumped all the fences perfectly. He had realised that it was not safe for him to argue with me. I made a big fuss of him, telling him how clever he was, patting and stroking him and demonstrating the different reaction he would get from me when he was a good boy.

After this *contretemps* at our first public outing we continued our training every day. Gradually we began to look like a combination working in harmony together. Chips had mastered the rudiments of dressage. But this was not the only aspect to which I paid attention. All the time I tried to feed him so that he would put on more weight, for he had become so very thin and poor after his cough when he had first arrived. I discovered that, no matter how many oats he was given, they made no difference to his temperament, and this delighted me, for it meant that when the time came for him to get really fit, I could increase his oat ration without the uncertainty as to how he would be affected. He was not a 'good doer', and it took me a long time to find out just how much he could eat and still be interested in the next meal.

After his morning work I would lead him out on a long rein, and while he grazed on the rich spring grass, I used to imagine our competing together against the best in the world. Had anyone told me then that these dreams would come true, I would just have laughed, and certainly no one else would have entertained the idea for a minute.

In the meantime, I carried on with my secretarial work. In the late spring I was even coerced into visiting London, to inspect the various colleges and fulfil my mother's wish that I might emerge with a first-class secretarial degree, which would enable me to take up a post anywhere in the world. Luckily for me, it was decided that none of the colleges were without drawbacks, so once again I returned home to continue as before, with the compromise of taking private shorthand lessons to increase my speed.

Spring passed by, and with its going I found myself profiting by the experience of attending my first horse trials. I went to the Gisburn event as a spectator and I learnt a great deal there. I saw that the standard of dressage was not high and even at Chips' present standard we would be more than competitive. It was the cross-country that I needed to think about. Once we got home again, I searched everywhere for similar obstacles.

One such venture almost brought my hopes to a violent end. We were hacking quietly in the country behind the town, and passed through a farmyard, only to be confronted by a stream. There was a bridge, a rather rickety wooden affair, but even this path was barred by high gates on either side, well chained to discourage would-be negotiators. The stream was only narrow, and from the bank one could see the stones on the bed glinting through the water.

I decided that here was yet another opportunity to test Chips' obedience, and accordingly walked purposely towards it. Patch trotted gaily through and up the bank on to the other side. We followed, but at the edge Chips gave an enormous leap, obviously hoping to make the bank without getting wet. Alas! With his front legs just striking the opposite bank, we performed a very ungraceful backbend and were both precipitated into the stream. The clear water began to turn an ominous black, and I scrambled out in horror, feeling the tug of sucking sand. I looked round at Chips, to see that he too realised the danger and had begun to thresh frantically in an effort to make the bank. In vain, I tried to guide him, and made another mistake by leading him towards the bridge. Had I only known, safety lay in the other direction; for this murderous patch of quicksand was only twenty yards long on either side of the bridge. But I didn't know and was trying all I could to help Chips out. His frantic struggles grew more and more feeble, until after a last tremendous effort, he turned around and would try no more. By this time all the cows in the field had come to investigate and were clustering round me on the bank adding to the general melee. Patch shot across the stream again and chased the cows – distraction was complete.

I was now in despair, I knew that single-handed I could do no more, so I ran breathlessly across two fields to the farm calling as I went for the farmer. Imagine my dismay when I learnt that the tractor was out. I gasped out our plight and gathering ropes we raced back to the stream to find Chips still in the same place but sinking slowly into merciless sand.

Luck turned, for suddenly the tractor appeared and joined us at the water's edge. The ropes were secured to its tow-bar, but Chips was so far embedded that the only places left to put them were round his buttocks and under his tail. It was too dangerous to put any round his neck, except for guiding purposes, as any sudden strain would result in its breaking. The tractor's wheels slowly began to turn, and the ropes grew taut. There was a tremendous sucking noise, and Chips regained a little hope.

He started to thresh about again, and might even had made the bank, but the ropes, strained to bursting point, snapped, and he rolled back into the stream, sinking again. This time he really surrendered and would have put his head under had I not supported it while new ropes were put round him. A second attempt had to be abandoned as his legs had become wrapped under the edge of the bank. At last he was in a position for us to try again, and this time, with everyone straining in a final effort, he rose slowly out of the stream and was dragged to a safe distance up the bank.

There he lay, covered in slime, so weak that he was unable to move. We stood looking down at him, fearful that even now all was not well, and that perhaps his struggles had resulted in a twisted gut. After a few minutes, however, he began to recover, and suddenly jerked to his feet. He was trembling all over, and I started to lead him gently forward. With every step strength seemed to return, and I began to hope again. We were about three or four miles from home and faced with getting back as soon as possible. There was nothing for it but to walk, and off I set leading a filthy and very dejected Chips beside me.

The farmer telephoned the news home, and my father set off in his car to meet us. He took over, and gallantly continued the walk homewards, while I drove on to change my dripping clothes and swallow scalding sweet tea. Then back I went to relieve my drooping parent, who climbed thankfully into the car and went ahead to put down straw and take up the bran mash I had left cooking. At last we reached the stable. By now Chips had dried out and had stopped trembling. We rubbed him down, and finally left him warm and well wrapped up. My worst experience was over.

But still there was the worry that he might develop pneumonia, and we passed the next few days on tenterhooks. Nothing happened, and I slowly began to realise that physically, at least, the episode was to have no evil result.

The experience left him with a very natural dread of water. Although, as the months passed by, he seemed to recover a little confidence, he still remembered that day, and I was always worried about what would happen when we were faced with a water splash in a cross-country course. Horses never forget, and it is very hard to erase a bad memory once it has formed.

Chips certainly seemed to bear a charmed life, for there was a second occasion on which he nearly lost it in a dramatic fashion. Before we moved to the Hall stables, he had a loosebox in the carrier's stable. This building is railway property and flanks the goods yard which was the actual line terminus before St. Annes and Blackpool were big enough to warrant railway service. The goods station is neighboured by the usual Railway Inn with a stable yard at the rear rented by the owner of the beach ponies. There are two entrances to the yards separated only by the 'local', and easily confused by anyone but the Lythamites.

At the time of this incident, one of the old beach ponies had to be destroyed, and following the usual procedure, the knacker was instructed to collect the animal and take it away. Chips was enjoying his afternoon siesta and there was no one about when the tumbril pulled to a stop outside his loosebox door. The driver let down the ramp and looked round the stable for a halter. Then he opened the box door, and was about to lead Chips out, when the carrier's friend and occasional helper happened to look in. Seeing that I was not present at this strange scene, he decided to hold things up. But for this lucky intervention Chips would have been fed to the lions in Blackpool Tower.

The season progressed, and we competed in various ordinary shows as a practice for the horse trials which were to follow. Our local pony club, only recently formed, decided to send a team to the Area Trials, and every week we would meet to practise and choose a team. Chips and I were included, and qualified to compete in the championships by leading the associates – over seventeen and under twenty-one years of age. The Team was beaten by an infinitesimal margin into second place. This augured well for the future.

Meanwhile I continued in my task of improving Chips' dressage, with Henry Wynmalen's book, *Dressage,* as my guide. Whenever it was time to go a stage further in Chips' training, I would consult Mr Wynmalen's book first, and then try to put into practice what I had learnt from his theory. I found his advice invaluable and continued to use it as a reference for many years.

Later on, I met the Wynmalens at one of the events and was asked if I would like to stay with them for some dressage training with Chips. I felt immensely honoured and jumped at the chance. Henry and his second wife, Juanita, lived at Kingswood House, near Wargrave in Berkshire. I had never seen such a beautiful house. It was surrounded by their own paddocks and a most appealing stable yard where they had run a stud for some time. The Wynmalens were extremely fond of Dachshund dogs and had several of them who followed Henry everywhere.

My stays there gave me a different perspective on life. I adapted very quickly to my new environment and I was particularly impressed by its large and elegant dining room, with the magnificent long rectangular table and eight comfortable high-backed chairs, valuable centrepieces with flowers arranged with flair and an expert eye for colour, snowy white napkins of the finest linen, silver flatware and crystal glasses. My bedroom was huge, and I could look out from its two large windows and admire the paddocks laid out before me with their covering of green lush grass, the well-kept post-and-rail fences, and the private garden with its manicured lawns and wonderful old trees which surrounded the property and protected its privacy.

Some years previously Mr Wynmalen had invited the Pullein-Thompson sisters to Kingswood House and Josephine wrote about this experience in their joint autobiography, *Fair Girls and Grey Horses*. She describes how they were allowed to ride Basa, his grey Hungarian-bred Arab stallion, who was highly intelligent and beautiful, almost house-trained. At the time Mr Wynmalen was at the vanguard of the post-war adoption of the continental style of horsemanship in England. Later Josephine was to breed and train an eventer called Rosebay, who had been sired by his stallion, Basa.

I found it very easy being taught by Mr Wynmalen. I was on the same wavelength as him and had no difficulty in understanding what he wanted Chips and me to do. Juanita would join us and these lessons were almost joyous for us all. I produced what was wanted and retained the knowledge. I understood why the movements should be done this way.

Mr Wynmalen was Dutch by birth and was a great all-round sportsman. He flew airplanes to the extent of being an ace racing pilot, and he had taken part in all the big international races across the world over various distances with great success and distinction. He had won the Paris to Brussels race. He also raced very fast motorcars and was a first-class shot. He and Juanita spoke several languages and I felt very inferior. I had never met a man with so many gifts.

Our first official horse trials were in Yorkshire, at Hovingham Hall, the Worsley's home. This was to be our first real test, and for weeks I had been carrying on with Chips' dressage training and getting him fit for the anticipated rigour of the cross-country course at the Trials. I had overheard a trials' competitor say at the Gisburn event that she worked gradually up to one and a half hour's road exercise daily before a one-day trial. I checked with Margaret Hough and she confirmed that she also went up to one and a half hour's road work when she started a new season. After that she continued increasing the time by a quarter of an hour as she completed each week of work, with a maximum of two hours daily. I thought about this and decided that as Lytham and all the surrounding districts were so flat that Chips would have to do an extra half an hour's road work to reach the same level of fitness that a horse working in undulating country would achieve. I began to map out a weekly programme with the addition of half an hour's dressage to be worked on immediately before starting out on the road work.

I had sent in my name to the British Horse Society months beforehand, so they might forward all of the trials' schedules. Soon I received a copy of the current Novice Dressage Test, which all the competitors would perform at the trials that autumn. The tests were issued at the beginning of a season, and revised from time to time as the necessity arose. There was the Novice, the Elementary, and the Badminton Test. As it was Chips' and my first attempt, I had to learn the Novice one, for we were entered in that class, while the more experienced horses and riders would compete in the open class and do either the Elementary or Badminton Test.

The Novice Test included nothing Chips could not do already, I had only to master the sequence of movements and make quite sure it was all fixed in my mind to such a degree that when the time came to perform I could concentrate on Chips' execution of the various movements, and not have to be worrying the whole time about the next sequence. The dread of forgetting any part of the test acted as a real spur to my learning it absolutely by heart. I drew little sketches of the arena and its lettered markings and recited the test out loud as I pretended to be riding it with my pencil.

To practise the test on Chips was out of the question, as one of the gravest faults in a test is for the horse to anticipate the next movement. A horse learns very quickly, and after going through a test a few times has it firmly lodged in his memory, presenting untold difficulties to the rider. Naturally, I was able to incorporate some of the movements in our ordinary dressage work without doing any harm, but only once did we go right through the test before the competition.

Mummy was getting more and more nervous as the days passed. She watched my professional approach and how much work I put in on Chips, his feeding, grooming and exercise, never being deflected from our programme whether the weather was fine or foul, and clearly intent on only one thing, a good performance at Hovingham. She knew, as we all did, that Chips and I had not had anything like the practice we should have had over fences and we both had the demons of the quicksand lurking in our minds for any water fence on the course.

Mummy was a stalwart Roman Catholic and she knew that St Jude was the patron saint of hopeless causes and she was absolutely convinced that I came into this category, so she went to church, unknown to any of the family, and had a word with St Jude. She struck a deal with him that if he looked after me and Chips at Hovingham and saw that I won, then she would give the Church the price of a mass, which in those days was five shillings. She would also place a thank you to him in the personal columns of the Daily Telegraph the following day acknowledging what he had done. I had no idea of this pact she had made at the time.

At last it was time for us to travel to Hovingham for the Trials. Margaret Hough was giving us a lift in her horsebox. So, Chips stood next to Bambi, who had so recently won the Badminton Trials. We arrived at Hovingham late in the afternoon of the day before the trials, and after introducing the horses to their surroundings walked round the cross-country course on foot.

The weather, for some weeks past, had been atrocious, with the result that the course was waterlogged, in some places to such an extent that some fences were quite unnegotiable and had to be cut out altogether. Some of the open competitors decided not to risk their valuable horses, and it was under these conditions I was to make my debut.

Clouds were low and threatening, and as Chips and I entered the dressage arena to perform our test, sure enough the heavens opened, and the elements combined in an effort to disrupt Chips' equanimity. But to no avail. On he went with his test, as if such disturbances were everyday occurrences. We always did our dressage training regardless of wind, lashing rain or sunshine and he knew that I would not accept the excuse of bad weather for him to vary from the standard I knew he could produce. Here he showed, for the first time, the temperament which was the foundation of his successes.

At the end of the dressage phase, we found ourselves in the lead, and I was highly delighted. The show jumping phase was next, and the course fairly difficult. Chips and I jumped round, knocking two down as we went, but we were still in the lead of the novice class, with the last phase, the cross-country, still to do. We stood at the start, and I wondered what the next few minutes would bring as far as the two of us were concerned. The flag fell, and we started out on the two and a half-mile course. I could feel Chips was in great heart, and we sailed over the fixed rails, brushwood and other obstacles with no trouble at all. We passed through the finishing posts well within the time allowed, so even gained bonus points. Our first venture into the field of horse trials had ended in triumph.

How proud I was of Chips, and especially delighted with his behaviour on the cross-country phase, for he had betrayed no fear of the treacherous conditions and was not unduly distressed with his effort. As we bowled along homewards in the horsebox, I began to dream happily of our programme for the next season, determining to spare no effort.

Before our season came to an end, there were still the Pony Club Championships at Tetbury in Gloucestershire. I was representing the Fylde and District Pony Club. We had no horsebox of our own at the time, so transport was a major problem. Some friends came to the rescue with the generous offer of their trailer and truck, and our enjoyment was greatly increased by their company when we traveled south to the championships. The meeting was to be held in the grounds of Highgrove, at that time the lovely home of Colonel Morgan-Jones. In 1956 it was sold to the Macmillan family, and in 1980 it was sold to the Duchy of Cornwall and became famous as the trysting place of Charles and Camilla. We spent the day before the event getting Chips accustomed to the place in which he was to perform, and also giving ourselves shocks by walking round the cross-country course, and discovering the various pitfalls into which I could so easily fall on the next day.

Unknown to me, these championships were visited by the top echelons of dressage judges and members of the Horse Trials Committee in the hope of spotting new talent for the future. I was oblivious to everything but the necessity of doing my very best to win for my club. I was also entirely unaware at this early stage of my eventing career, that the majority of southerners were somewhat disdainful of anyone coming from the north. At this point I was unaware of the undercurrents of social prejudice. I was now eighteen and a half years old and could hardly wait for the competition to begin. The show jumping arena was on good going but the show jumps themselves looked somewhat flimsy, in an old-fashioned type of way. I would have preferred them to be more solid. We walked around the cross-country but compared to Hovingham it was relatively easy.

Zero hour approached to find us ready and waiting at the side of the dressage arena. Chips went through the day in splendid form, and by evening we found ourselves the new Associate Champions for 1954, but by only one mark from Joan Perry on Farewell. My confidence in Chips' future received yet another fillip, when Colonel Williams, whose wife was the leading Grand Prix dressage rider for Great Britain came over to congratulate me. His wife had been judging. He said that he thought that Chips was a horse fit for horse trials proper. His wife had told him there was a new girl and a horse from up north. Another judge, Victor Saloschin, from Tetbury, was also full of praise for Chips' performance and I could hardly believe all the forecasts by the equestrian experts when we read the accounts of the championships in *The Field*, *Horse and Hound*, and the newspapers.

I knew nothing of the manner in which the prizes were to be presented, and had been told that only riders, and not their horses, would be required when all the results were known. Chips, therefore, was rugged up and put into the trailer, while I, thinking there was plenty of time, left bowler, stick and gloves reclining in the front of the truck. The inevitable happened; loud speakers suddenly came to life asking that all winners should ride into the ring to receive their awards. Panic resulted. In our hurry to saddle up Chips again, my hat was forgotten but at the last minute, attention to its absence having been drawn by a disapproving official, it was collected from the truck and hurriedly stuck on my head as we filed in. In due course, to my horror, photographs appeared in national magazines showing me grinning inanely with my hat sitting rakishly on my head.

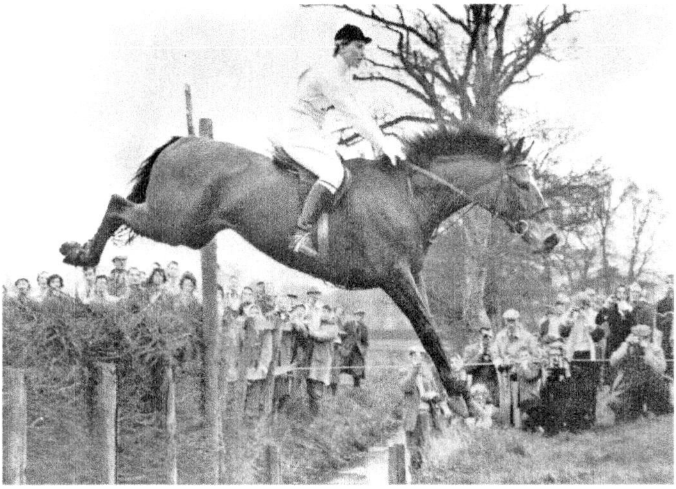

Chapter Five – Meeting the Stars

Chips and I were now on the ladder to success, but still the rungs above us seemed to stretch interminably upwards. His efforts for 1954 were now over, and our two friends undertook to drive him north, while my parents took me to Windsor where I was to join the horse and riders already in training for the European Trials to be held at Basle in October. As I mentioned earlier, Margaret Hough and I knew each other and when I first heard that she had been invited to train for inclusion in the British Team, I had leapt to the telephone, and offered to act as groom to Bambi, so that I might gain every little extra bit of knowledge at training headquarters. Hence our journey to Windsor, where I looked after Bambi, and watched and listened as the potential members of the team underwent their rigorous training.

Every day I was in contact with the leading event riders, people upon whom I had looked as almost demi-gods; Colonel Frank Weldon with his famous Kilbarry whose triumphs were almost legendary, Bertie Hill who farmed in Devon and was a beautiful natural horseman riding Crispin, Major Lawrence Rook with Starlight, Ted Marsh who loaned horses to the British Team and the two women Diana Mason with Tramella, and Margaret with Bambi. All of them were first-class, so I watched everything they did, and learnt much.

I did not know it at the time but some of those men who I regarded as 'demi-gods' were to persecute me relentlessly as I moved up in the sport. The real reason why the men had decided that no woman was ever as reliable on a horse as a man was that they feared the woman might get 'the curse' on the day of the cross-country. They were also inculcated with natural chauvinism that was a social feature in those times.

The Harewood Trials were to provide a testing ground for the Team, and we traveled north from the Royal Mews a few days before they were scheduled to begin. The weather was ferocious, and we shivered and shook as wild gales played havoc with everything. Accommodation for the grooms had been provided under canvas, but as Margaret wanted to be near Bambi, we were quartered in a caravan near the grooms. I had never slept in one before, and it was not an experience I wanted to repeat. The caravan itself was pleasant, but the gales proved too much for it, and at night I tossed and turned sleeplessly while my 'house' rocked, creaked and groaned to the accompaniment of the whistling wind outside. The last straw came when one night I became conscious of something pushing up and down against the wall outside. I was terrified, and did not dare go out to investigate, until I realised my visitor was none other than a cow!

The opening day of the trials arrived, with a high wind still blowing strongly. We learnt that during the night the tent in which the girl grooms were sleeping had been ripped from its pegs, covering its occupants with yards of canvas – they had to move to the fodder rooms and loft instead.

But the funniest sight of all came when I was returning with Bambi after she had done her dressage test. The stables and grooms' quarters lay down in a valley and were approached from the main arena by a rather steep hillside. As I walked down towards the stables, I looked at the scene, and then looked again – for, out of the men's changing-rooms, a tent similar to the one already blown away, were yards and yards of streamer-like objects dancing merrily in the wind. I drew nearer, and almost collapsed with laughter when I was able to identify this phenomenon as – toilet rolls! They must have unrolled as the wind howled through the tent, and now flew everywhere as if in feverish protest.

I felt that there was a distinct aura of sadness and gloom around Harewood House. I found out later that the Princess Royal, the eldest daughter of George V and Queen Mary, had been forced into a marriage in what was considered a suitable dynastic match, with the elder son of the then Earl of Harewood, a much older Royal suitor. On the evening of that marriage, Mummy's school had taken the unprecedented step of saying a prayer especially for the Princess Mary in her distress.

The Team horses were competing here *hors concours* – they were ineligible for prizes, and next day ran simply over the cross country phase of the speed and endurance test. All went well, but the choice of our representatives for Basle narrowed. The last day with its show jumping round came and went, and soon the horses were loading into the horseboxes to travel back to the Royal Mews at Windsor, to complete their training. I was looking forward to the trip to Basle enormously, so it was a nasty shock for me to learn of the decision to take only male grooms over to Switzerland. I was also upset that no Selector or the Team Captain came to me and explained why female grooms were to be excluded. My presence at Windsor was now superfluous, so home I went, consoling myself with the thought of all I had seen and heard during my time with the Team.

Meanwhile Chips had been enjoying a rest, but on my return, this had to come to an end. I began to put into practice all the theory I had amassed during my time at Windsor. I found a marvellous jump on the beach – the jetty, along which our fishermen trundle their little carts full of nets and other tackle. It was a wooden structure, very wide, and at various heights along its length. The drawback was that the tide covered it once or twice a day so that the boards became very slippery for some hours after the water had receded. I decided that this could be yet another lesson for Chips, and after convincing him that it housed no demons likely to jump out at him, I turned him round and set sail for it at full speed. Chips' eyes nearly popped out of his head. He suddenly realised that he could not possibly stop in time, and would have to get over somehow. Legs waved in mid-air as we took off, and I felt his hind-legs strike wood with a hollow ring as he used the boards as a spring to complete his leap. We landed on the other side, safe and sound, and after that it became one of our ports of call, until we were able to fly over it with comparative ease.

Then there were the boats, dotted invitingly all over the beach, where trusting fishermen had left them out of reach of the tide. Not so out of mine, and we became quite adept at leaping all sorts and sizes, until the fishermen, viewing this practice with jaundiced eyes, decided to subject their boats no longer to such frivolous treatment. Muttering at such lack of confidence in our ability, Chips and I had to turn elsewhere for our cross-country practice over strange obstacles. But as the days grew shorter, I found it took me all my time to exercise Chips and look after him properly, and still continue to act as secretary to my father.

One Saturday morning, I was reading *Horse and Hound* as usual, and suddenly out of the print leapt an advertisement for two people to make up a car-load traveling to Basle for the European Trials. Here was an opportunity too good to miss, and my enthusiasm was such that it overcame all opposition. It even caught the imagination of John, my brother, for he too decided to accompany me. Immediately after breakfast I telephoned the advertiser, and arrangements were made then and there for John and me to join the party. Again, my good fortune had its drawbacks, for in return I was persuaded by my parents to apply for various secretarial posts. Letters were sent off, extolling my virtues, while I tried to look forward only to my visit to Switzerland.

Chapter Six – Swiss Venture

It was mid-October when John and I traveled to London, there to meet our fellow-passengers for the first time. We all joined forces at one of the car hire offices, for we were to travel abroad in one of the firm's Vauxhalls. I had volunteered to do some of the driving, and accordingly undertook a short test in London's traffic to prove my capabilities before being let loose on the Continent.

At last we were organised, and with luggage piled on the roof and overflowing from the boot, the six of us squeezed into the remaining space and set off along the road to Folkestone, and the Channel crossing. The next day found us on French soil, driving towards the frontier. We were still on the road the following morning, and the strain of continuous driving was beginning to have its effect on our host. A change-over was obviously necessary, so John who had just acquired his licence, was only too eager to volunteer, and soon we had rearranged ourselves for traveling on through the countryside. We were shaken out of our apathy a few miles further on by the noise of furiously blowing whistles, and, craning our necks in an effort to see out of the back window, we espied an agitated gendarme waving his baton in the air and dancing excitedly in the middle of the road. His comrade rushed to a motorcycle propped against the wall and in a whirl of dust chased us.

We decided to stop, and waited for the storm to break. Apparently, John had contravened one of the French rules of the road. One of the gendarmes jotted down John's details in his little notebook. We drove on a couple of thousand francs the poorer, and fearful for John's new licence.

The first two days of the trials were devoted to the dressage phase, and our Team of Kilbarry, Crispin, Starlight and Tramella gave good accounts of themselves. Tramella, in particular, performed a brilliant test, and at the end of the first day stood at the head of the Individual placings list. This mare was only 15 h.h. and a bright bay colour with four white socks and a blaze. She was out of a Welsh pony mare of unknown breeding, by the Thoroughbred, Tramail. Bambi also went well, but her score did not count for the Team, as she was competing only as an Individual entry, quite apart from our Team of four.

We walked round the cross-country course before it was time for the speed and endurance to begin, and found it very difficult and over undulating terrain. It has since been said the Basle course was as hard as any of those for the Olympic trials, and certainly the obstacles looked forbidding and would obviously take their toll on the competing horses and riders. There were several big drop fences, and some of the worst obstacles lay towards the end of the course, where tired horses and riders would be more likely to come to grief than if they had encountered the obstacles earlier in the course. There is a horsey saying that if a rider is approaching a frightening fence, they must throw their heart over first. There were a lot of competitors at Basle who forgot this maxim and paid the penalty.

The steeplechase course was different from any of our national ones, for at Basle its fences were not all brushwood, but included a wall and even level-crossing gates. This meant it had to be jumped at a slower pace.

There were a lot of falls. The fences towards the end of the course caused much trouble, and we saw an unpleasant accident when a German Team member somersaulted over the fixed rails with his horse and both lay winded on the ground. The horse recovered first, and jumped up. He was held by a steward while the rider sat up dazedly, and eventually returned to full consciousness sufficiently to be put back on his horse and pointed in the direction of the next fence. His face was streaming with blood, for he must have landed on his nose, but he courageously continued along the course towards the finish, although I'm sure neither he nor his mount would remember much of those last few minutes of the phase. We saw Bambi and Starlight at the same fence, the former refusing before jumping it perfectly, and the latter getting over miraculously without a fall.

Then on we went to the wide water-jump, which had a concrete bottom. Some of the horses were being pulled up as they approached it and asked merely to step down and walk out the other side, for it was only shallow. There was a roar of applause as the gallant Crispin came towards the jump; still full of running, he leapt cleanly over it, and galloped on towards the finish, up the long steep hill at whose top lay the final phase of the run in.

I began to realise how important it was for a horse to be very fit. It was obvious that a great many of the falls and refusals were brought about simply because the horses were too tired to produce the necessary effort. I realised, too, that one had to produce a horse fit enough, not only to finish this gruelling speed and endurance phase, but to do so in such a way as to be ready on the next day to jump round the show jumping phase. To many people this show jumping appears very 'small beer' when compared to the jumping proper, but it is incorporated in the trials to show that after a day of tremendous effort, the horse is still capable of jumping carefully around a course of jumps.

The show jumping at Basle took place on a racecourse outside the city and began in the early hours of the Sunday morning. Crowds were enormous, and we were completely wedged together in the stand. Our discomfort was worthwhile however, for we saw the British Team continue to display their all-round superiority and become the new European Champions. The first three places were taken by Crispin, Kilbarry and Starlight, and Bambi and little Tramella were sixth and seventh.

On my return to England, there had been various replies to my inquiries to the advertisements, and I found myself caught up in a whirl of interviews. All of them were in the south of England, so I arranged to meet my potential employers before going home.

The first interview was in London and I punctually presented myself at the reception desk of a first-class hotel. I was informed that 'His Lordship' had not yet emerged from the dining-room; in the meantime 'Milady' was asked if I would care to wait in the drawing-room. My sudden ascent to the nobility so amused me that the ensuing interview seemed relatively unimportant. I left with the matter in abeyance, until I had presented myself to other would-be employers.

The next interview was for the post of personal secretary to the owner of a country estate in the south of England. She had varied interests, and here there was the added attraction of my being allowed to have Chips with me, as consolation. However, it turned out that I should have been buried away in almost nun-like surroundings, so regretfully I decided that this was not for me either.

The third was for a somewhat similar post, although this time as personal secretary to the principal of a very sedate young ladies' finishing school. Here again I could take Chips, for riding was on the curriculum and it was considered that I might even come in useful as a chaperone when the girls went out for a ride in the surrounding countryside. I would also be required to pass on my knowledge of shorthand to the girls, and also deal with considerable French correspondence. This prospect did not altogether deter me, but the presence of a pet budgerigar worried me considerably throughout the interview, and ultimately, I decided that rather than spend the next year or so always on the alert, I would forfeit the place.

The next few weeks I spent in agonies of anticipation awaiting the results of the interviews, but fortune decreed that I was not to be offered a position and there was no change in my way of life. I was still free to pursue my dream. Chips and I continued our training.

Chapter Seven – Riding Cross-Country

November brought the Duke of Edinburgh on a visit to some nearby factories, and rather than join a gaping crowd I decided to ride Chips out of the borough boundaries to the road along which the Royal car would have to pass. We did not have to wait long before the long procession of cars appeared in the distance, and from the grass verge Chips and I had a grandstand view. As Prince Philip's car went by, he leant over to take a closer look at the horse which was one day to become quite familiar to the Royal family. Then he was gone, and Chips and I turned back to continue our daily exercise.

By now, the weather had begun to show its wintry teeth, and my dressage field became useless. I found a flat piece of land near the beach, the property of the corporation, and happily continued to work Chips there until one day I was approached by a friendly constable and warned of the proposed 'raid' the next day. Apparently one public-minded citizen had seen our activities and reported us to local police headquarters. So, forewarned, Chips and I took our exercise in the hinterland, while patrol cars converged on my improvised dressage field, only to find their 'bird' had flown.

Soon after this, another accident curtailed our activities for some time. One of the fields in which we worked backed on to what is known locally as 'Green Drive' – a mile-long tree-lined path barred to motor traffic. Leading from the field on to the drive there was a narrow iron gate. I decided that we should jump it. We had already negotiated a hedge between fields and a nearby water trough, then I turned Chips towards Green Drive and the iron gate. It was over four feet high and surmounted by unprotected blunt spikes – for the iron struts of the gate were laid vertically. I must have been out of my mind even to contemplate such an obstacle, but I didn't stop to think about it, with almost fatal results.

We approached the gate. A pace or so away from take-off I knew instinctively what was going to happen, for I felt Chips slip on the wet turf. He took off right under the gate, managed to clear it in front, but brought down his hind-legs on top of the railings. Somehow one of the iron spikes became wedged between shoe and hoof, and I picked myself up to find him sprawling on the ground with one leg still anchored to the gate. Luckily the shoe gave way under the strain, and his leg was free. He scrambled to his feet. My heart leapt to my mouth as I saw the glint of white bone through one of the gaping holes. I did my best to staunch the blood before leading him back to the stables, calling at the veterinary surgeon's house on the way. He came at once, and in no time, had cleaned out the wounds and inserted several stitches. Throughout Chips stood like a lamb, though I felt sure he must have been suffering agonies. I cursed my own stupidity, but it seemed as though Chips too was determined that the two of us should make good, and in ten days the stitches came out, and we were able to start work again.

By this time John had left school and was considering the regular army as a career. He had emerged from Ratcliffe with colours for boxing, cricket and rugger, and every weekend during the season, he appeared as full-back for the local Fylde Club rugger team. We would all troop to the ground to watch him, and both John and I joined in the various social activities which took place in the club-house from time to time.

The New Year came in, accompanied by the usual festivities, and a fortnight later, Chips and I left for Leicestershire to gain cross-country experience by hunting. We stayed with the Edlins at Thurnby, and Chips lived next door to our one-time stallion Algayam. Using Thurnby as a centre, we were able to hack to most of the local meets, and our weeks there flew past with my first experience of hunting proper. Chips was a superb hunter, and we had tremendous fun out with the Fernie, Quorn and Cottesmore packs. We had one particular long run, towards the end of which I found myself alone but for the Huntsman, whose horse was visibly flagging. Another fence loomed in front of us. His mount refused, and as Chips soared over, I caught sight of hounds well over to my left. We turned towards them and raced up to a very big, hairy hedge with a gaping ditch on the take off side. At the last moment I saw a strand of wire in front of the ditch, but it was too late to stop, and as we took off I felt the tug of the wire on Chips' chest and closed my eyes anticipating the fall I felt sure would come. But the next moment we had landed safe and sound on the far side, and I was thankful that the rusted wire had given way to Chips' thrusting weight. His only marks were a few long scratches, and once back at the stable I washed them out and dabbed on antiseptic.

Sometimes it was too far to hack to the meet, and in those cases I drove myself there with truck and trailer. This was a fairly new acquisition, bought after the Pony Club Championships where we had been so impressed with the performance of our borrowed transport. We searched around and soon found a trailer. The finding of a suitable truck, however, presented a far greater problem, and our eventual purchase was a rather ancient model, whose components, I suspect, dated from the days of the first motor vehicles. It turned out to be far from road-worthy, and would develop all kinds of internal complaints, always at the most inconvenient times.

This particular day, I had bravely driven about fifteen or twenty miles deep into the hunt country. Leaving the trailer at the side of the road, I saddled Chips and trotted the remaining impassable half-mile or so to the meet. The weather was bitterly cold, and I had taken the precaution of covering the radiator with a muff. But this precaution was in vain; for on my return at the end of the day the engine would only splutter and wheeze dismally. However, after much labour, she did condescend to show a little life, and thankfully I let in the clutch, and we moved off slowly.

By this time hounds had been brought to draw a covert nearby, and a number of car followers were parked in a long line on my side of the road, necessitating my swinging over to the right to get past. The engine, none too happy in the first place, began to utter loud groans and creaks in protest, drawing many curious glances from the followers as we passed by. Half-way along the line, a car appeared in the opposite direction. Instead of controlling his impatience for a few seconds, the driver came straight on, and I was forced to brake violently. The engine uttered one final gasp and gave up the ghost. Now I was blocking all one side of the narrow country road, and nothing could get by until the hunt followers moved on. But they were utterly unconcerned about my predicament and continued to concentrate on proceedings in the nearby covert. The other driver got out of his car to give me advice on how to start the truck again. He then turned his attention to moving the line of cars farther along the road, and once his way was clear, he swept on without more ado.

I was left, weary and dejected, and worried too, that Chips might catch a chill. A cyclist and another driver offered to help, but eventually had to admit defeat. We decided that the only thing to do was to go in search of a garage mechanic. The nearest village was five miles back along the road, and here we drove in the other car, persuading the mechanic to return with us. It was dusk when we reached the truck and trailer, and while the garage owner and his mechanic tried to find what was wrong, I rubbed Chips' ears in an effort to keep him warm. At last the engine spluttered indignantly into life, and I was able to jump into the driver's seat and set off back towards Thurnby and a good night's rest.

Our time in Leicestershire drew to a close, and my father arrived to drive us north again. On the way home, the truck displayed more of its talents, and so horrified him that he determined to have a new engine installed immediately. This was done, but the attraction of truck and trailer had palled considerably after our experiences, and before long we were once more devoid of transport for Chips.

It was while I was hunting in the Midlands and John was busy learning to be a soldier, that there was a most fascinating development in the kaleidoscope of our family life. The weather had been particularly dreary and my father's business trips unduly prolonged, so that my mother had found herself housebound, and alone. Ordinarily she was quite given to enjoying her own company and would tell us that she needed the occasional spell of solitude to get her breath. But during the lengthy hiatus she found herself reading far too much and getting bored with humdrum chores and television. Not being the afternoon bridge tea-party type or given to good works or to sitting on committees, she cast about for some personal interest which would keep her from middle-age despondency.

In a matter of days, much to her own astonishment, she dumbfounded us all by becoming the owner of the smallest but prettiest dress shop in the town. This was the more amazing as she had never had any business experience at all, and certainly knew nothing of the 'rag trade'. But she had known where to put her hands on the right woman to run it for her. Certainly I was able, through this hobby of mother's, to buy many more clothes than I could have otherwise afforded; but I always had a feeling that, at the back of her mind, my mother had the notion that the shop could be a line of independence for me should my life with horses not work out.

Chapter Eight – My Way or No Way

The spring season of 1955 was on its way, and with the opening of the trials at Glanusk almost upon us, we bought a furniture van with a more amenable engine, and had it converted into a horsebox. We cut through the metal sheeting above the driving-cab and inserted two large windows, so that Chips could look out at the passing countryside. He really enjoyed his journeys in this box and majestically watched the changing scenes with the greatest interest. We traveled north, south, east and west secure in this truck. It was a very reliable means of transport.

By this time John had passed the Royal Commissions Board with flying colours and had joined his future fellow-officers as a cadet at Sandhurst. While he was starting off on his first weeks of strenuous training, my mother, father, Chips and I set out for Breconshire and the Glanusk Trials. The knowledge I had gained at Windsor with the Basle team, and the conclusions I had drawn from the trials themselves, resulted in my getting Chips into much fitter shape than he had been the previous autumn when we had made our debut. Then I had gone to the trials not realising that a horse should be galloped systematically in preparation for the cross-country. Now I understood the importance of these gallops and had ridden Chips accordingly at varying speeds and distances along the beach at home, pretending that he was a race horse out for his early morning 'pipe-opener'.

He now had four feeds a day, and I gave him carrots and brown sugar, in an attempt to persuade him to eat up. As his oat ration increased, and he became fitter and more lively it began to show in his general demeanour. He would pull the most awful faces at anyone daring to enter his box and wave a foreleg threateningly in the air whenever I was grooming him. He started to chew at his halter rope while I ministered to him and demolished several to show his displeasure when the grooming brushes tickled him. Several times he undid the rope and was then able to turn his attention to me, I would have to leap out of reach of his teeth and hurry to anchor him once more to the wall. But it was all quite harmless really, and if ever his teeth did make contact, no one was more surprised than Chips himself. I even encouraged him in his wickedness, for he was careful with me and so

I felt no compunction about it. It all contributed to his becoming a 'one man' horse, and this prospect delighted me.

We were staying quite ten miles or so from the Glanusk Estate in which the trials were to be held, for we had picked out a hotel at random from the guidebook, because it was able to supply a loosebox for Chips. The hotel itself was antiquated in the extreme, but the quarters in which Chips was to be stabled were in a dreadful state of disrepair and we were totally dismayed. After a hurried conference we jumped into the car and began a tour of the town in the hope of finding a more suitable loosebox, but after an hour or two's vain searching, we were forced to return and try to conjure up some semblance of stable order from the dim depths of the long disused building. At last it was done to the satisfaction of us all, and Chips was left to spend a night in complete darkness while we made our way into the hotel.

Upstairs the corridor floor resembled a switchback, and boards creaked alarmingly. My parents' room had an enormous four-poster, complete with tapestries and heavy curtains. It stood high off the ground, with ladder-like contraptions on either side. In one corner the gas meter had been tastefully covered over by a polished wood cabinet, fastened by lock and key. Our amusement was complete when my father found that the whole thing lifted neatly away from the wall, leaving the offending meter in the nude.

After we had arrived there a day in advance, there was plenty of time in which to inspect the cross-country course and make ourselves familiar with the terrain. One of its most terrifying features was a post-and-rails in front of a wide stretch of water. This was my worst nightmare!

I decided to look for some water near where Chips was stabled, so that I could gain his confidence for the next day. Soon I saw the glint of water and rode over to investigate. We found ourselves on the towpath of an old, disused canal, and peering over the edge, I decided that here was the very thing. I imagined it to have a solid bottom, and it therefore seemed to be just the ideal spot for practising. A most unwilling Chips was finally exhorted into taking the plunge, and suddenly we were in the middle of the canal with all the mud and silt of ages clinging to our skins. We were both terrified, remembering our last ducking, and splashed frantically for the bank, finally to emerge dripping with filthy water, and distinctly shaken.

Small wonder, next day, when after leading the novice class throughout two phases, Chips stopped at the water splash, and was only just persuaded to jump in time to escape total ignominy. We dropped to sixth place, and another bitter lesson had been learnt. The following morning, we returned to the scene of Chips' disgraceful exhibition, and jumped back and forth over the offending obstacle until he was flying over in a carefree manner – his confidence, completely restored, as far as that particular jump was concerned.

It was too far to go home in between the trials. I stayed at Northleach for a week, and then traveled on to Ascot, there to wait for the opening of the European Horse Trials which were being held that year in England at Windsor. The Stowell Park Trials came first, however, and with the prospect of the Windsor dressage test in view, I had entered Chips here in the open section, for which the same test as we would all be doing at Windsor was to be used. After lying second to Tramella, the then leading British dressage exponent of the trials world, we reaped the reward of my folly by our one and only elimination, at a fence relative to the open cross-country course alone. His three refusals were followed by a standing jump, so I knew nothing of our complete disgrace until we finished the course. Both my parents were all for giving up the idea of even going to Windsor now, but the arrangement had been made long ago for my stay in Ascot. So, Chips and I traveled on south, and were soon installed in the Ascot stables, to spend the next three weeks in hard training.

While at Ascot I was forced to lock Chips up one day, as a bloodstock sale was in progress in the same yard, and potential buyers, scanning their catalogues, would keep peering into Chips' box, obviously thinking him to be one of the sale horses, and asking me the oddest questions. As the sale went on, I felt I had only to turn my back and Chips would be led out under the auctioneer's hammer. To set my mind at rest I rushed round searching for a lock and key, and was at last able to leave with Chips behind the comparative safety of a locked door.

This period also marked the occasion of my first meeting with Mr Goodfellow and his family, who later became great friends with the Willcox clan and most enthusiastic supporters of what Mr

Goodfellow christened the 'Fish and Chips' combination. A month or so before setting out on our spring tour, I had noticed an open invitation which appeared in the current edition of *Horse and Hound* to riders and their horses to visit Mr Goodfellow's farm near Reading, and to practise over his cross-country course. Ascot was not very far from the Goodfellows' farm, so I decided to take Chips there for a schooling session, and accordingly telephoned the farm to settle on a mutually convenient time and date. In due course Chips, myself and Jean, the girl who was later to take over the duties of groom to Chips for the trials, climbed into the horsebox, and drove to Wick Vale.

After taking various wrong turnings, and generally losing all sense of direction, we eventually arrived at the farm gates and were met by Mr Goodfellow. Chips was unloaded and saddled up. I walked round the course to learn the way, and then jumped into the saddle and after a preliminary canter we set sail for the first fence. This he climbed over with no great enthusiasm, and before long was refusing point blank to negotiate a water-jump in the wood. There was barely any space in which to manoeuvre, as almost the whole course was in a little spinney, and only the keenest animal will jump round first time without any trouble. Chips, quite obviously, was neither keen nor feeling very obedient that day, and after second and third attempts, equally unsuccessful, the three human elements joined forces in an effort to dominate the will of one very stubborn horse. Flanked on either side by a two-legged terror waving a branch, Chips was rushed at the obstacle again, but to no avail. He still refused, and in so doing almost knocked over my partners. He was determined to have his way, and I was just as determined to have mine too, so battle raged under the trees until at last he capitulated and jumped. My triumph was short-lived, for the next minute he was repeating the performance at another unusual fence. His behaviour throughout our visit was quite disgusting, and when at last we put him in the box to drive back to Ascot, I decided to return at the earliest opportunity to make certain of his taking to heart a much-needed lesson.

The next day I drove to Wick Vale alone, and with Mr Goodfellow's watchful eye upon us, Chips and I proceeded to make our way over the course without further trouble, although not with any pronounced enthusiasm on his part. Our raised spirits were somewhat dampened by sudden torrential rain, and I rushed Chips back to the box while we waited for the fury of the storm to abate. The skies cleared at last, and we were able to emerge, and as I prepared Chips for the return journey, Mr Goodfellow wandered round the box and found that one of the tyres had gone completely flat. We unscrewed the spare wheel from inside the box, only to find it almost as soft as the punctured tyre, and the absence of a pump made it impossible for me to drive to a garage. Telephone calls resulted in the vague promise of a mechanic from the nearest garage, so in the meantime I was taken into the house, and met the rest of the family. I spent a most enjoyable hour with them until I was able to drive back to Ascot with Chips. I never forgot how kind the Goodfellows were to me that day, and it was that which laid the foundation of a friendship greatly cherished by my family and myself.

The chance of even acquitting ourselves moderately well in a three-day trial were slender, to say the least of it, especially after our recent form. My hopes were still lower on the day of the 'walk-round' when I saw the cross-country and steeplechase courses we were to negotiate, in addition to the energy-sapping roads and tracks and the run in, all of which constituted the second day's speed and endurance phase. The Windsor Trials were an International Meeting, and the entries included six Teams, each of which consisted of four members, the cream of their respective countries. Such was the competition Chips and I faced in our very first three-day trials. I wondered how on earth I had even dared to enter.

All the horses were subject to a compulsory veterinary inspection on the eve of the competition, but I was missing as Chips' turn to be examined approached. Colonel Babe Moseley, no doubt cursing the very fact of my existence, jumped into his car and raced in search of me, while I, utterly oblivious of the furore my absence was causing, made my way with Chips towards the inspection yard by a 'bridle' path. Meanwhile, Colonel Moseley had found my father and had learnt of my departure. He invited my father to accompany him back to the yard, driving there at record-breaking speed, only to find Chips and me placidly making our exit with a clean bill of health.

Later that evening I took Chips for a final leg stretch. There was plenty of exercising space behind the Stud Farm, where the competitors' horses were stabled, and soon I was wandering about on Chips with other riders working their mounts all round us. A little brook ran through the field, and here and there a clump of bushes formed a natural obstacle. I decided to jump over them once or twice, and was surprised when Chips firmly refused to co-operate, I became extremely annoyed when it grew clear that we were to have another battle for mastery, and both Chips and I were fighting one another furiously. My parents arrived, to view this exhibition with dismay, and for the next few minutes could do nothing but watch helplessly as slowly but surely, I gained the upper hand, and made Chips jump the obstacles and the brook several times. When at last I was satisfied, we were both terribly hot and extremely exhausted, so I dismounted wearily and walked Chips round for a while until we were more or less recovered, and were able to return dejectedly to the stable. I wondered how this *contretemps* would affect his outlook, and hoped it would have an impression deep enough to curb any untoward ideas for the speed and endurance day, and all those terrifying fences I had been shown.

Our own dressage test took place in the afternoon, and Chips seemed to go so well that I was sure he would get a very good score. I was extremely disappointed when the marks were announced, for we heard that ours were only fairly good, and later, with the judges' marking sheets in my possession, I was dismayed to find they were free from any comments which would have helped me to realise where we had made our mistakes. However, as far as the dressage was concerned in these trials, there was absolutely nothing I could do to improve matters. I could only hope to finish the next day's course and perhaps better my position.

My parents had seen nothing of the roads and tracks, so with the idea of refreshing my memory, we set off that evening along phase A in the car. Eventually we reached the steeplechase course and took up the next phase C, from the last brushwood fence. This time the path along which the arrows pointed proved more and more difficult for the car, as we pressed deeper into the woods, and inevitably our attempt at rivalling a Land Rover's performance in a mere saloon-car ended in disaster. We became well and truly stuck half-way up a leaf-strewn slope, and though we packed the tracks with branches and lumps of wood, and all got behind to push like demons, the car refused to move. It seemed as if we would have to abandon it and return for help.

Hope rose when we heard the whine of an approaching engine, and a powerful car appeared and just managed the ascent. Our plight was obvious, and had they only stayed to help, the car would most certainly have been set on its right track. However, they drove off with the off-hand promise of sending someone as soon as possible. Then two little boys arrived on the scene. My father sent them off in search of a spade with the promise of a cash reward, and in no time they had returned. Soon the mud and leaves had been removed from beneath the car's wheels and flat pieces of bark laid in their place. One of us sat in the driving seat to steer a way out, the rest placed their shoulders to the rear of the car, and with a few extra stone of our miniature Robin Hoods, the car lurched from its bed and came to rest on solid ground.

Competitors set off on the speed and endurance test at five-minute intervals. Chips and I started on the long, lonely ride and I was filled with an unswerving determination to finish the course – come what may! I had heard through the gossip network that odds-on were being offered against Chips completing the day's course. We had never jumped around a steeplechase course before, but my valiant horse galloped round the two-and-a-quarter miles circuit without a single penalty. We even managed to gain a few bonus points. As we flashed through the steeplechase finishing posts, to set off on the second roads and tracks, one of the spectators shouted to me that Chips' girth had come undone, and I looked down to see his safety girth flapping loose against his flanks. I had to stop and readjust it, and then we were off again at a trot and canter for the next six-mile phase.

We came to the starting posts for the cross-country. This was to be the real test, with those thirty-odd solid, fixed obstacles ahead of us. As we galloped into the first fence I was threatening Chips with extinction if he dared repeat his Stowell form. At the seventh fence, a giant tree-trunk, I lost my whip in the effort of getting over, but there was no time to retrieve it, and on we had to go. We sailed over enormous parallel birch poles with a deep ditch between them, and then ran into our first trouble at the culvert fence, where one had to jump down a drop of four feet into water, cross the culvert and leap up three and a half feet to get out. Chips' eyes nearly jumped out of his head at the sight of this atrocity, and he hovered on the brink, taking a step backwards before jumping in. This constituted a refusal. Then we went on until we caught up with one of the Italian Team who had set off five minutes ahead of us. He had obviously run into a good deal of trouble, and his horse was exhausted. At that time, I didn't have sufficient experience, so I held back waiting for him to go on, whereas in actual fact I should have pressed on.

As it was, Chips lost all his impulsion, and when I decided we could hold back no longer, we had to jump one of the most difficult fences on the course, the fearsome sand quarry. In the ordinary way it would have been terrifying, but after the mix-up with the Italian, it was even worse. Chips came to a stop at the rails which stood at the top of the quarry. It was a wicked jump and had already caused much grief. On our second attempt we managed it. Then we had to slither down the quarry side to the bottom, and finally leap over the single fixed pole erected on the far edge of the top and step into space. Five feet down we hit solid ground again, and then we were off towards the next fence, over which Chips soared easily. Out of the corner of my eye I noticed a still shape lying to the right of the obstacle's landing side. Later I learnt that this was the body of the horse which had been killed falling at the fence.

Our third refusal was due to bad luck, for we met a simple pile of cordwood absolutely on the wrong stride, and it was impossible to jump from right underneath the fence. Chips did make a half-hearted effort at getting over but succeeded only in trapping one of his front legs in the wire that bound the logs in place. Someone rushed to the rescue, and quickly disentangled the leg, no doubt expecting Chips to struggle frantically in panic. He was quite unmoved, however, and while he was being freed, he stood on his three legs and calmly surveyed the scene taking the opportunity to recover his breath. With four legs on the ground again, we turned for another try. This time we flew over the cordwood and pressed on towards the end of the course.

A violent hail-storm scattered the crowds, as we approached the Irish bank, five feet high, with a three feet six ditch on the take-off side. Chips and I struggled on, up and over the bank, and away to the water-jump. The hail pelted into our eyes as we galloped straight into its fury, and I could not even see the water. Luckily my sense of direction must have been good that day for we arrived at the right fence, and then turned homewards with the storm at our back. We leapt the last few obstacles, and started off on the run in, finishing our first gruelling speed and endurance test a few minutes later. When at last I was able to get off Chips and 'weigh-in,' I had collected so much moisture from the hailstones that I weighed five pounds more than at the start of the day. I was absolutely soaked to the skin and was walking with my boots half-filled with icy cold water.

Arrangements for the parking of competitors' cars had gone somewhat awry in the stress and strain of the day, with the result that ours was miles away. I was therefore rushed over to perform the operation of stripping in a friend's sportscar, a TR2. But first my top boots had to come off, and my mother couldn't manage it. She went over to a group of young police-officers and asked for their help. She was all but drowned under the flood of ensuing offers, but the sergeant, 'as a married man', fixed the rest with a stern eye and bade them remain where they were while he followed her back to the car and released me from my clinging boots.

Anyone who has been in a TR2 will know how little room there is in any case, but my performance as a strip-tease artist was a work of art. At last I sat in nothing but my skin with my mother's coat wrapped round me to preserve my dignity. Without more ado, I put down a bare foot on the accelerator and shot back to the hotel six miles away for a quick bath and change, while Chips returned at a more sedate pace in his horsebox. When I went out to see how he was after his efforts, I saw that one of his knees was beginning to swell slightly as a result of a bang he must have had somewhere on the course. Apart from that, he seemed none the worse, and after Jean had rubbed him down, fed him and bandaged his legs, we were able to leave him for the night.

Early next morning Jean was out walking Chips round the yard in an effort to wear off his stiffness before the veterinary inspection at ten o'clock. We were now standing thirteenth, an improvement of one place from the dressage tests, and had only to jump round the show jumps that afternoon. Chips was passed by the vets, and later in the day we rode in the parade of competitors still remaining in the event. In the show jumping we had one fence down, and retained our position of thirteenth. So, then we filed into the ring again with the other prize-winners to receive our award. There were fifteen awards, and as we stood in the line I realised that apart from Mrs Boon with Neptune, and myself, all the rest of the places were taken by the male riders, and all except one were members of the different Teams. I was proud of my horse, having so neatly confounded the critics. Now, I was looking forward to the autumn season, when we would be able to compete with a far greater confidence in our ability.

Chips' other life. Here he was during his summer retreat, with Patch and me offering him his daily ration of oats.

In training at Windsor Great Park before Turin. Also, in the picture are Virginia Gilligan on Jungle Queen, Colonel Weldon on Kilbarry, and Major John Birtwhistle on Delagyle.

Chapter Nine – European Championships

The early summer months passed by while Chips lazed in the field enjoying his well-earned rest. I helped with secretarial work and in the house, or just idled about at home. I went to the Sandhurst Ball in June and in the same month received a letter on behalf of an Australian asking if I would consider selling Chips. I refused but was delighted to know that evidently someone else was beginning to realise his potential.

Then came the request from the British Horse Society that I should lend Chips for training as a 'possible' for the Olympic Team. I remember how very flattered all the family were, but my better judgement won, and ultimately, we all agreed it would be most unwise to let the BHS have him. I wrote back to the committee and explained that as Chips was my one and only horse, I felt it was rather too much to expect me to give him up for the long training period, especially when I considered him not yet at his peak, and therefore more liable to be confused by a strange rider giving him orders in a different way from mine.

Soon it was time to think of making up a pony club team again, and I began to help the local committee in their task of selecting the four representative members. This year I was ineligible for the team event, for my win of the Associate Championship the previous autumn barred me from competing in any of the Pony Club Area Trials, though we had automatically qualified for the Championships in the separate advanced event.

I also began to think it would be good policy to look for another horse, a young one, which I could be training to take Chips' place in a few years' time. But all the horses I went to see were of no use to me as far as the trials were concerned, and when the time came for me to bring Chips up from the field and start work once more, he was still the only one.

We had decided that perhaps our disappointing dressage marks at Windsor were due to some underlying fault about which I knew nothing. With this in mind, Chips and I went for our first professional instruction to Captain Goldman at his school in Cheshire. He was a brilliant teacher, and under his instruction we improved hugely. He worked unceasingly on my dressage, and we concentrated largely on aiming to perfect the execution of all movements which were incorporated in the current Badminton Test. The weather was hot, and in the indoor school it was almost unbearable. Chips' backing became much better, and this was important for the test demanded a difficult 'see-saw' of six paces back, four paces forward and six back then halt. It sounds easy but to do this well is extremely difficult, for the horse must rein back in two-time and take exactly the number of paces required, no more, and no less, if he is to gain high marks for that particular movement.

Each of the thirty-odd movements was marked out of six. It would be the easiest thing in the world for the rider to accidentally give a wrong aid to the horse, perhaps through nervousness, and thereby lose precious marks in a trice. One of the hardest parts of the test was a half-pass from one of the quarter-markers to the centre line, straight up the line and off it again at the other half-pass to the quarter-marker at the top end of the arena. It is difficult enough to do a correct half-pass at the trot, but in asking us to trot on up the centre line before the second sideways movement, the test designers had shown their cunning. From their vantage point at the top of the arena, the judges would be able to see with ease whether or not the horses were correctly bent as they approached the centre line. They would also be able to see whether or not they came up the line with hind-legs following straight behind the forelegs or with hind-quarters still at an angle, before moving away from the line again in a half-pass. If the horses were not absolutely straight on the centre line, marks would be subtracted accordingly, and all these points, on top of the usual pitfalls of loss of rhythm, balance and cadence throughout the test made the whole thing very difficult indeed.

The instruction we received from Captain Goldman brought its reward, and at the first autumn trials at Malton in Yorkshire we finished first by a wide margin. The next event was the Harewood Three-Day Trials and we drove over the Yorkshire moors to join the other competing horses in the stables on the Princess Royal's estate. To my amazement Chips settled down almost at once and began to eat everything before him. This was a tremendous relief for until then, whenever we had taken him away from home, he had gone right off his food and worried me terribly with his self-inflicted fasts. Perhaps the bracing Yorkshire air tickled his palate, but whatever the reason I could not have been more pleased to see him looking hopefully around his manger.

Dressage day arrived, and Chips was in a very good mood, joining me in my determination to produce a first-class test for the judges. We did just that and created something of a furore by leading the field and standing above Tramella, unbeaten in Europe for the previous two years. Overnight we stood first in the individual placings, but by the next evening we had dropped down to fourth, due entirely to my lack of cross-country riding experience.

We had jumped into the cattle-crush far too fast. It was a combination fence set at an acute angle, and Chips failed to negotiate the turn for the second half. I had to circle round inside the crush before we were out and galloping on to the next fence. I made another mistake at the tunnel obstacle. The sun had been shining strongly as we shot into the tunnel, and both Chips and I were temporarily blinded by the sudden plunge into semi-darkness. Not unnaturally he almost collided with the sandbags which constituted the fence, and we had to turn again for a second attempt. All the other difficulties and hazards of the course provided Chips with no trouble at all, and we leapt the last fence safely before passing through the finishing posts, with the loss of those forty penalties for the two refusals – though these we offset with our score of bonus points for being well within the time allowed.

With a final clear round in the show jumping phase on the last day, we finished fourth with Colonel Weldon and Kilbarry, Michael Naylor-Leyland and Bright Prospect, and the Irish Copper Coin ridden by Penny Moreton, standing above us. It had been a most marvellous event for there I received one of the greatest thrills of my life. After emerging from the dressage arena, I found myself surrounded by members of the British Horse Society committee, and to my utter amazement was being asked to join several other riders at Windsor to train for possible inclusion in the Team to go to Turin in October.

I went home from Harewood in a daze, and should have traveled to the Pony Club Championships at Kenilworth with Chips the following week. However, my nervous system must have sustained too great a shock, for I had an attack of tonsillitis, and instead of racing madly across country to the Midlands, I reclined in bed at home. I recovered swiftly, and the date for assembly at Windsor found us in the Royal Mews with the other horses and riders. There was another woman, Virginia Gilligan with her mare Jungle Queen; together with her friend who was acting as groom, we were quartered in a flatlet on the castle walls, and joined up with the rest of the party for work during the day and meals at one of the local hotels.

The training was the greatest fun, although very rigorous, and the lungeing work in particular was most exhausting until one became used to it. We were placed on a lunge horse without either reins or stirrups, and jolted round for half an hour's agony at a time, while a continuous flow of instructions as to what we should be doing with every part of our anatomy issued relentlessly from our tormentor in the middle. I was most bewildered by it all at first but then, as it became more familiar, I began to enjoy myself, and was even able to listen properly to the various instructions without worrying that I might fall off.

Chips and I were also introduced to something new, the cavaletti. This was an exercise over poles, done at the trot to encourage the horse to use his back and neck in the correct manner, resulting in a more supple and handy animal. The poles are placed on stands only twelve inches from the ground and at equal distances. Then the horse is trotted towards the line of poles and, if he performs correctly, will continue to trot in two-time as he negotiates the 'grill' with a swinging back and suspended action. It is most spectacular. Both Chips and I enjoyed the work tremendously and he soon became extremely proficient. Then there was the dressage, which we did under the guidance of Mrs Williams, who spared no effort to improve us all, soon finding out our weak points and working on them until they became better. The test for the Italian trials was a new one, so that also had to be memorised. It included something I had not taught Chips, the transition into a canter from a halt. He was very dim about this at first and I almost strained my leg muscles giving him the aids which I had to emphasise in the extreme before he began to realise what I wanted him to do. To give him his due, though, once he knew what he was asked to execute, he produced transitions with no intermediate walk steps, calmly, with the aplomb of a veteran.

We took long rides and galloped the horses once or twice a week, until they were absolutely fit. Chips was always the last off the field at the end of a gallop, for he was not by nature a very fast horse, and indeed confounded everyone at the trials by recording such good times. The secret lay in the fact that he never altered pace even when going into a fence, and his long, sweeping and regular stride only served to give a very deceptive impression to the casual observer.

Our five weeks of training passed quickly. Before the composition of the Team was finally decided upon, we all traveled up to Warwickshire to compete in the Wellesbourne One-Day Trials near Stratford-on-Avon. The ground was almost bone hard, but it did not deter Chips in the least, and he followed his good dressage score and clear show jumping round by a fast cross-country, to win the open class by a fair margin. The victory clinched the possibility of our being included in the Team, and that evening it was announced that my other team-mates would be Michael Naylor-Leyland with Bright Prospect and Commander John Oram with Copperplate.

The three horses were to be flown to Italy from Blackbushe Airport, and after getting ourselves up at five in the morning, we all arrived on the tarmac in plenty of time to load the horses and luggage into the plane. The nose of the plane yawned open to admit them, and with surprisingly little trouble, we had them inside and ready for take-off. The rest of us piled into a compartment to the rear of the horses, and there I stayed throughout the flight. It was Chips' first time in the air, but he behaved as if it were an everyday occurrence, and displayed little or no interest, except to show his disapproval when one of the other horses began to thresh about in panic.

We had been told that the plane would touch down at Paris and Marseille *en route*, but the weather was so good at Blackbushe that it had been decided to call only at the latter. After an hour's flying time, a little note was handed down from the cockpit and we read that in view of the perfect conditions, the plane would fly straight to Turin. Soon we were approaching the Alps, and from my porthole it looked as if the peaks reached almost to the sky. I thought our little plane would never ride above them, but as we flew on, I realised we were following the Brenner Pass, so the towering peaks still lay on either side, until we emerged over the Lombardy Plains and saw industrial Italy lying at our feet.

We were hours ahead of schedule and touched down at the airport outside Turin just as everyone was enjoying a siesta. Not a soul of the official welcome party was there, so we allowed ourselves to be persuaded by one of the airport staff to delay unloading the horses at least until the Press arrived. We all trooped into the lounge, and were presented with strong black coffee, which I loathe – and waited there for the arrival of our reception committee. At last a lone photographer arrived, soon to be followed by a huge Army truck which was the horses' transport to their stables. I remember thinking that they would be lucky to emerge unscathed from such a death-trap, but in actual fact they all traveled quite happily as far as the race course at Mirafiori, where they joined the other competing horses.

The remaining half-dozen humans were escorted to an enormous charabanc waiting in the park outside the airport, and we followed the horsebox at a discreet distance. Our horses were stabled next to those of the German Team and were all in a range of boxes away from all the noise and bustle of the main yard. The quarters in which the grooms were to be housed were rather primitive to say the least but our three cheerfully made the best of their surroundings, while we left them to it to drive on to our sumptuous hotel. It was right in the centre of Turin, and outside hung the flags of the six nations competing. There were Teams from France, Germany, Italy, Turkey, Switzerland and Great Britain, and I soon discovered I was the only woman competing against all-male opposition. Four of the Teams had their full allowance of four members with the best three scores to count. Great Britain and France had only three, which meant all of them had to finish every day to keep their country in the running for the Team award. The rest were Individuals. All the competitors stayed in the same hotel, and my disappointment was acute when, after looking forward enormously to seeing a real, live Turk. I found them not in the least extraordinary – and without a fez between them.

The inspection day dawned, and all the Teams and their entourages piled into the coaches and set off for the racecourse where our second day's speed and endurance test would start. The first roads and tracks led us out of the main gates and for a mile round the walls of the race course. Then we re-entered the course to start the steeplechase phase of two-and-a-quarter miles over a course which twisted like a corkscrew and required absolute concentration, if one were not to take a wrong turning in the excitement of the moment. On to phase C, more roads and tracks, and these took us through the streets of Turin, along slippery roads and over main crossings and tramlines.

The distance of this phase was nearly ten miles, and only towards the end of it did the going give way to softer tracks and a few grass verges.

Even so our path led over a swollen river by means of a wooden bridge, then being assembled on the spot by the army – it rattled alarmingly at our tread and swayed ominously. By this time, despite the anticipated terrors of the cross-country phase, I was starving, and looked forward to finishing these roads and tracks when the usual snack was to be distributed. To my utter dismay the vehicle bringing our lunch had not arrived in time, and so, still fasting, we were shepherded on along the course for the cross-country.

It was situated on very uneven terrain, and many of the fences were sited just round a bend in a woodland path, hidden from view until the very last second – devilish obstacles designed by wily course-builders. Halfway round the course the food van caught us up and I was able to eat. In a better frame of mind, we all set off again chatting amiably to each other in between fences and exchanging opinions as to how the different obstacles should be taken on the day. As usual, I was striding along in the advance party, and we set such a good pace that from time to time the official in charge of the walk-round had to call a halt to enable the few stragglers to catch up the main body, when he would explain the intricacies of a certain fence and how it would be judged.

On we would go again, but in time our headlong rush was brought to an abrupt stop when we came face to face with a shallow river. The course could clearly be seen stretching onwards from the far bank, so quite obviously we had to get across somehow. A tree-trunk formed a very unsafe bridge, and a few brave souls balanced a precarious way across. The rest, however, decided to wade over, regardless of getting feet wet. I was hovering on the edge looking for the shallowest place, when one of the German Team, Otto Rotte, caught sight of me, and whisking me up, waded across, to deposit me dry shod on the opposite bank. Had he only known then how we should be standing after the dressage phase, perhaps he might have ignored this gentlemanly instinct; but obviously he was not prone to psychic flashes, and I was able to continue on the walk-round in comfort.

That evening the Mayor of Turin gave a marvellous drinks party in the magnificent Town Hall. As the only girl competitor, I was encircled by all the town dignitaries and soon blushing with the compliments delivered with the famous Italian charm and the sincerity of big brown eyes. I was young and inexperienced and had no idea of how to deal with such attention, but I did think that perhaps I could take to this sort of thing if only I had the practice.

The dressage tests began at eight next morning, so I had to be up very early to ride Chips from the stables to the Football and Sports Stadium, in the confines of which the dressage arena had been placed. It was on the edge of the grass centre of an athletic running track, and one had to ride down a sloping wooden platform covered with green matting, when the time approached to do the test. Chips went down the platform, and we trotted around for a minute before the bell rang as the signal for us to begin. We cantered straight as a dye into the arena and came to a four-square halt and gave a low bow to all five judges. Throughout the test Chips did his very best. One judge's marking sheet, where they comment on the overall test, had just one word: "Superb". I was proud of Chips and relieved that I had not let down the team. Our performance was not equalled throughout the day, and at the end of this first phase we stood at the head of the International field, with my German Sir Galahad in second place, four points behind, tying with a compatriot who also had the same marks. Our team was in second place with a total of 288.8, only 10.4 points behind the Germans. Usually they lead the rest of the field by an impressive margin after the dressage phase, but they were not as reliable on the speed and endurance.

Again, in the evening we went out, for the British Team had received an invitation to dine at the house of Umberto Agnelli, owner of the giant Fiat works. We drove the thirty miles west of Turin out towards his country residence near Pinerolo, and drew to a halt outside the steps leading up to an imposing entrance. We passed through the ornate rooms, footmen with powdered wigs and frogged jackets flanking the walls. Then we were greeted by our host and introduced to his house-party guests. We talked for a while over cocktails, and then went into dinner, taking our seats round an enormous table laden with the most beautiful crystal wine glasses, elegant silver flatware and exquisite china. The room was lit entirely by candles, hundreds of them, which threw our shadows on to the walls and gave an almost ethereal quality to the surrounds. It was late when we eventually took our leave and returned along the winding road to Turin.

I was relieved to think that at least we didn't have to ride competitively on the morrow, which was set aside for looking over the cross-country and the rest of the speed and endurance course for a second time. Michael, John Oram, Colonel Weldon and I walked the cross-country again in the afternoon, and after poring over my map of the course for a while, I decided that there was a possibility of a shortcut between fences.

Michael and I started off from the fence in question, he followed the marked path and I walked along a track which I believed and hoped would save us considerable time on the course and thereby add valuable bonus points. We called out to each other as we went and after a few minutes I emerged about twenty yards from another fence. I was delighted until Michael appeared and we realised that by following my track I had missed out one of the fences. It was very sad, so after all the trouble, it seemed as if there were no alternative but to follow the marked route like everyone else.

In the evening another cocktail party was held, this time in the ancient home of the Marchesa di Medici di Vascelles, in whose estate the cross-country phase was being held. In these charming surroundings we wandered from group to group, sipping cocktails and nibbling at the various delicacies and gazing at the paintings around the walls by the world's leading artists, priceless art treasures and brooding hunting trophies, killed and stuffed through the generations. Then we took our leave, and I spent the night tossing and turning in my bed, thinking anxiously of the course which faced Chips and me on the next day, and hoping and praying we would not let the Team down.

Heavy rain had fallen before the start of the trials. Each morning since our arrival, we had been rising to find everything shrouded in grey mist, which disappeared only when the sun grew strong enough to melt it away. The officials were anxious whether it would clear early enough for the speed and endurance test to start which is scheduled at eight o'clock in the morning. There were still traces of mist when Chips and I set off a few minutes after eight. We went at a brisk trot through the race course gates on the roads and tracks, phase A. Visibility was no more than a hundred yards, but this was enough until we started on the steeplechase phase, when at full gallop I found it difficult to follow the correct course and see the turning flags in plenty of time. At one of these I also might have carried straight on, and lost valuable time marks, had it not been for Colonel Ledgard, one of our British supporters who having foreseen this possibility, had posted himself at the appropriate stop.

As Chips and I thundered towards him he pointed the way with brandished shooting-stick, and so I was able to turn at once instead of searching in the mist for the correct course. I pulled Chips up from his headlong gallop as we passed through the B finishing posts and started on phase C; then I allowed him to walk a few steps until he regained his breath, and soon was able to urge him into a trot when his second wind brought renewed vigour. A Land Rover - bearing my parents, Colonel Weldon and Major 'Pop' Rankin, the vet, passed me with the news that we had gained maximum bonus points over the steeplechase course. With this to give us heart, Chips and I pressed on along the roads and tracks, negotiated the army bridge safely and finally reached the finish of the phase to find the occupants of the Land Rover and our grooms already waiting for us.

In the few minutes I had to spare before my scheduled start of the cross-country phase, Chips was hurriedly sponged down so that he might feel fresh for his forthcoming exertions. Then I jumped on again, and we were flying towards the first fence of this all-important phase, Chips in blissful ignorance of the hazards which lay ahead, and I determined not to fail the Team by being the weak link.

We set off clearing each obstacle and then came to the giant bullfinch, which had really intimidated me on the walk-round. Unlike those we had encountered in home trials, this one looked quite solid and stood over five feet high. It was approached by a long steep slope, and right from the top I concentrated on making Chips go faster and faster, gaining impetus at every stride to take us over the fence. We simply shot towards it and took off in a tremendous leap. It seemed as if he had not touched a single twig, and he must have jumped very, very high, for it felt to me as if we were never going to touch the ground again. When we eventually landed on the far side, it was with a most awful thud, as if we'd dropped from the skies. Then we were over the last fence, and after that it was an easy matter to gallop round the run in and complete the course.

It was all over for Chips and me. He was led away to be cooled down, while I weighed-in and then Colonel Weldon bundled me into a waiting car, to be rushed back to the start of the cross-country phase to tell my team-mates how certain of the fences had ridden, and perhaps give them some confidence from knowing that Chips and I had finished without any trouble. My part was over, and there was nothing more for me to do but watch the other competitors at some of the fences and wait until the marks were announced.

And at the end of the day the British team had moved into first place. Our total penalties for the first two days were 135.22, Germany in second place on 321.78 and the only other team to finish, Switzerland, on 721 points. And to my complete amazement – and everyone else's too, I suspect – Chips and I remained at the head of the Individual list by a margin which allowed us to hit one fence on the next day. In the show jumping phase of the trials, a knock-down constitutes ten penalties, so I could actually afford one fence and 7 time penalties to hold my place, but would possibly lose it if we had two down.

That evening, as we went down to dinner in the hotel, I was touched by the generosity of the other Team members, for as a tribute to my good fortune, they all rose to their feet cheering and clapping while I made my way rather sheepishly to our table. It was a really kind and generous gesture and is typical of the spirit in which these Trials were run.

At the veterinary inspection next morning, all our three horses were pronounced fit, and at the scheduled time all the remaining horses and riders in the trials presented themselves at the race course, where the final phase was to take place. It was a Sunday, and with the attraction of racing after the close of the trials, the crowd was enormous. The fact of my being the only woman in the competition had fired the imagination of the Italians, and when Chips and I had actually held on to our lead after the cross-country, they had become quite fearful lest we should do something silly in this last phase and spoil everything. It was comforting for me to know that I had friends in the stand who would be joining me in willing Chips not to knock down the two fatal fences.

The show jumping was not in reverse running order as it is nowadays, and I was the second to go around and could not know how the others were going to jump and had to perform as if they would go clear. I must not hit those two fences. Number five was a combination of three elements, and as we jumped the last part of it I heard a sickening thud behind which meant one down and ten penalties. We could afford to hit no more, and in my determination to clear all the other fences on the course I steadied Chips at every jump, making quite sure that we came up to the take-off on the right stride. All the people in the stands held their breath as Chips and I crawled slowly round the remaining fences, and then we had landed safely over the last one. There was a tremendous cheer.

We had done it after all, but sure enough our slow pace resulted in a few time penalties, so that with the ten for knocking down the fence our penalty total for the round was fourteen. The lead was secure now even if the others were to jump clear rounds, but in actual fact none of our close rivals did so, and there, had Chips and I hit another fence after all, we should still not have lost our lead. Michael, John and I held on to the Team placing. So, I was absolutely thrilled and could scarcely believe our good fortune. It seemed almost too good to be true. We were all ushered on to the race course again, to be presented with the Individual and Team awards. I had to climb on to the top step of a wooden rostrum in front of the stands, and I remember thinking at the time – suppose my breeches split in the effort! – for the steps were steep, and my breeches were on the tight side.

However, nothing like that happened to spoil the moment, and there I stood on the top step, while the band played the National Anthem and the Union Jack unfurled from the mast. It was my proudest moment, and although one day I hoped to ride again for Britain, there was never to be for me a more poignant space of time than those few minutes I spent alone on the victor's rostrum.

I was too young in those days to understand how lonely is the pinnacle at the top of one's profession. The full extent of the worst of human nature – jealousy and malice were still a mystery to me. I was young, female and the best, and consequently the old men who ruled the sport in those days would jealously guard their province. But I can look back and recall the feeling of pure and heady joy to be the winner. I didn't know the cost of winning those gold medals.

All the Italian crowd were delighted in my triumph and were as whole-hearted in their praise and congratulations as only the Latins can be. But a more sober note introduced itself, with the approach of someone detailed to ask whether I would consider selling Chips to the Italian Olympic Team. The offer made was extremely tempting, indeed I felt that no horse could be worth such a price; but if I did sell, then it seemed to me that it would be tantamount to my contributing in part to the aid of Britain's rivals in the field for Olympic honours, and this would never do. On top of all this, there was also my obvious reluctance to part with Chips, who meant so much to me. And it was quite unthinkable that I should leave Italy without him after all, he had done for me there. But against all this was the habit of years, the training which had taught me not to let heart rule over head. I kept thinking of the risk I took every time Chips ran in one of these competitions. One false move over the fixed cross-country fences and the asset of my horse would become a liability. Doubts raged within me, but in the end, I came to the right decision, and it was the heart which conquered.

Our win had also started up the controversy as to why a woman was not allowed to compete in the Olympic Games and, as the next ones were due to take place in Stockholm, 1956, the very next year, I thought that Chips and I might have something to contribute to this argument.

That evening there was the most splendid reception in the Club Torino, which had once been the Russian Embassy. Everyone was in the jolliest of moods, the champagne flowed, and even I was persuaded to take a glass, which to my utter surprise I quite enjoyed, for until then I had been strictly teetotal. As the winner of the Trials, I was toasted in champagne, and was introduced to many of the Italian nobility who were present in force. I must have been in a daze that evening, for later I could scarcely remember what had been said and whom I had met. The Club itself was a beautiful building, superbly decorated throughout, with all the former glory of its ambassadorial days still preserved. In an aura of excitement and delight, the last hours of my visit to Turin drew to their triumphant close.

The horses were to travel back by rail and sea, and in the morning my parents and I decided to go down to the station and see them safely on their way. Chips was in fine form and obviously none the worse for his exertions. The grooms and the vet, were to travel with the horses in the railway van and had been provided with great hampers of food for the journey. Then the three of us traveled back to England by train and boat, staying at Paris overnight where I received another delightful surprise in the form of a huge bouquet of red roses which were awaiting my arrival at the hotel. They were from the members of the French Team. We took Daddy on a sight-seeing tour of the city, but he, the Philistine, was utterly unimpressed, and said it reminded him of Manchester.

We crossed the Channel in stormy seas, settled ourselves in the Golden Arrow, and eventually arrived at Victoria Station where, to my embarrassment, photographers were already waiting. As they took their shots of me pretending to be emerging from the train, I could see other passengers nudging one another and whispering, "I wonder who she is". It's odd, I suppose, that at that point I didn't mind how many photographs of me were taken when I was on a horse, but on my own two feet it was quite a different matter. At that time, I was still so very young and shy and not at all worldly.

The horses were to arrive at Folkestone, and we drove down in time to watch them being swung off the boat in the most alarming manner. One by one, they were brought out of the docks, and led into a horsebox to be driven away and dropped off at different points. We were all staying at Ascot for the night, and soon had Chips settled in the same loosebox he had occupied during the European Trials at Windsor the previous spring. Next day I traveled up to London to appear for the first time on television. It was just a flash interview on one of the sports programmes, with Bill Allenby talking to Colonel Weldon and myself about our recent trip, but even those few minutes seemed most nerve-wracking and I felt very nervous while we were on air.

At last we arrived home. How glad I was to have a little peace and quiet after the hectic weeks we had spent away from Lytham. Chips went out into the field for a long rest, and we spent the next few months bathing in the aftermath of glory.

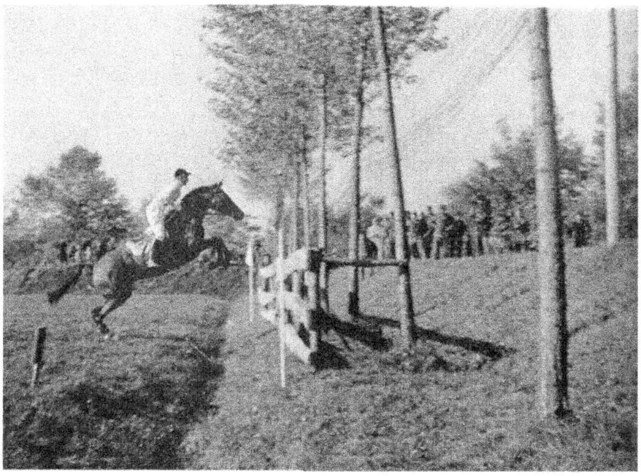

The International Horse Trials, Turin, 1955. Chips and I set out on the second day's speed and endurance test.

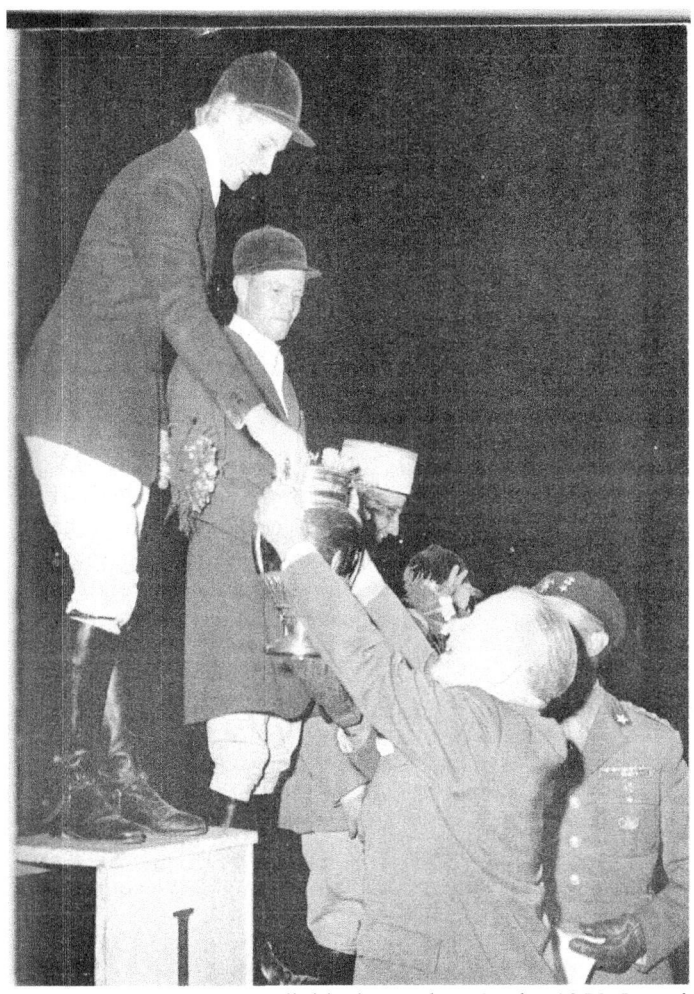

Presentation of the Individual awards at Turin, 1955. I received the winner's trophy from an official. August Lutke-Westhues looks on.

Chapter Ten – Losing Chips

Returning from Turin I again took up the hunt for another horse, but as before, met with no success until in Yorkshire I saw a seven-year-old gelding with the most enormous 'pop' in him. He was not a big horse, but had a great turn of speed, and so I bought him, naming him Ripalong. While Chips was continuing to languish in the field, I worked hard on this new acquisition, trying to make him relax and stop fighting against me. His head was never still, and he had only one pace a fast jog, punctuated by leaps and bounds, ever ready to fly off at full speed. I spent weeks calming him down by lungeing, and teaching him from the ground to trot, walk and halt as and when he was told, using my voice as the aid. Then I started work on his back and have never had a harder job in terms of producing a steady head carriage. Eventually, the continuous routine must have told, for he suddenly became much better and a few weeks later I could rely on his keeping his head still. He was a horse needing plenty of work and I began to wonder how on earth I could manage when the time came to bring Chips in and start his training again.

Around this time, I traveled up to London to attend a 'Young Celebrities Night' at the Forum Club. Princess Marie-Louise was present, and during the evening I was presented to her and she asked all about my Italian trip and the trials there. She was charming to me, and though she was obviously not at all well, she took the greatest interest in all the guests, and made a delightful speech about youth and sport. It was a memorable occasion and one of the last of her Royal Highness's public appearances.

The only person I knew there was Dawn Palethorpe, who was one of the top show jumpers at the time. We discussed the difference between her sport and mine and thoroughly enjoyed ourselves. Her family's business was the biggest sausage producer in England and she was related to Ted Marsh, a very keen eventer, whose position as third generation head of the family firm of Marsh and Baxter guaranteed the sort of lifestyle anyone would envy.

Ted Marsh was well known in the eventing world for having the most beautiful horses, which he was always willing to offer to the British

Team Selection Committee when they were having difficulty in finding a good horse for one of their male riders before one of the big international events. Ted had an old-fashioned hunting seat when riding. Although he had a full-time trainer, Major Jim Russell, a huge estate on the borders of Staffordshire and Worcestershire littered with purpose-built cross-country fences, a state of the art indoor school and a fine collection of show jumps, he would just miss getting into the top places in competition.

I had already overheard gossip that his wife was not the type one would have expected. I was not sure what to make of this. He was charming, erudite, polite and softly spoken. He was greatly respected in the business world, was a Justice of the Peace, and became Chairman of the Farmers Union. He was also a great shot and very keen on running his farm and estate at Kinver and his house and garden in Anglesey to the highest standard. He was reported to be very good to all his employees. And perhaps more relevant, he was said to be keen on the ladies in a very gentlemanly way.

I had seen him at my first three-day event at Harewood, when he had led in the dressage and ended up fourth, and where Chips had been the subject of much debate. I had returned to the stables before the show jumping and had been surprised and horrified to find two men in his box looking distinctly acquisitive. I recognised them immediately as Mr Marsh and Major Russell. With no premonition whatsoever of what lay in the future between myself and this man, I squared up to Mr Marsh and with courage borne of fright, that he might take Chips away from me, I asked them what they were doing in Chips' stable. Probably being accustomed to being welcomed with open arms in circumstances like this, with the neon pound signs ringing up in the owner's mind, this clearly took Mr Marsh by surprise, but he quickly collected his wits and apologised for not finding me first. I told him that Chips was not for sale and was nothing like the type of horse he liked and, please, may I get on with plaiting Chips for the show jumping. They left, and I muttered away to Chips while I plaited his mane. Then I forgot all about Mr Marsh and went up to the main ring at our first 1955 Harewood where we jumped a clear round.

Our first appearance at Badminton was to be in 1956. On the first of January I brought Chips in from the field and started working with him. We needed ten weeks of dressage and road work to be fit enough to be riding to win in our first event of the season at Stowell Park Trials. Last year we had been eliminated there and I was determined to succeed this time. Then we needed a further four weeks to gain the extra fitness needed. So that left the next two weeks for walking exercise on the roads to strengthen up and harden Chips' legs. First on the agenda was clipping off his long woolly winter hairs. I always looked forward to the metamorphosis clearly to be seen once Chips had come in and got tidied up.

The problem of where I was to put him became paramount. We had only one loosebox in the local carrier's stable, and while we had just one horse this arrangement had suited us very well, for it meant that if I had ever to go away from home for a day or two there was always someone to look after Chips. With the advent of a second horse, we had to look around quickly for somewhere with two boxes, and ultimately the question was solved by the generous offer of the boxes at the Hall. Within a few days we had moved back to the old yard in which I had already spent so many happy days when we had the ponies and the Stud.

Our training programme was pinned on the wall of the stable, with a pencil beside it which I used every day, drawing a line across the page as we completed that day's required work. Sunday was rest day and I always had to go to Mass at the Catholic church with Mummy, and John, but not Daddy. We still did most of our dressage work on the beach and we also galloped across the sands. We would fly along the length of the beach between Lytham and Blackpool, just short of the Blackpool promenade. Several years later Red Rum would be galloping in the same place, under the watchful eyes of his trainer Ginger McCain.

Then I decided to go once more to Captain Goldman's school, where we spent a further week preparing for the coming spring season. Just before the opening trials meeting, we had the additional advantage of going over from Holmes Chapel to Cholmondley there to ride over the discontinued trials' course. This practice was a great help, and we went on to compete at the Cottesbrooke and Stowell Park Trials with great success. At the latter Chips was in winning form, and there beat the great Kilbarry for the first time in a season, which was to result in tremendous rivalry between these two horses. However, this rivalry was nothing compared to the very strained relationship between Weldon and myself that was to develop over the years.

I was staying with the Bakers, whose daughter Sheila had been at school with me, and as Chips needed so little 'riding in' before a dressage test, I had decided to drive him over to Stowell in the horsebox, allowing about an hour before we were due into the arena for our test. We were in the heart of the Cotswolds, and the land rolls over hill and dale as far as the eye can see. I had been staying here for more than a week, and during this time the horsebox had not been used at all. In the interim period the battery must have run down, or something gone wrong, for the engine seemed reluctant to start and was wheezing and puffing up the enormous hills.

We crawled up on the main road from the village, and I uttered a sigh of relief as the road sloped away in front of us. Alas! It was short-lived, for the next incline proved too much altogether for the box, and we came to a shuddering halt. Rather than delay any longer, I jumped straight out of the driver's seat, pulled down the ramp and led Chips out. Precious time was running short, and I was in agonies of apprehension lest we should arrive after our number had been called. Frantically, I saddle and bridled Chips, jumped on his back, and at a trot which would not have disgraced an American Pacer, we set off along the hard roads in the direction of Stowell. We arrived with minutes to spare, so were able to regain a little breath, but I had worked myself up into such a state that I was quite sure I should never remember the test, and certainly be quite incapable of producing a good one.

Luckily the trials were running slightly behind schedule. We had a few minutes' grace, and that was enough for us to regain scattered wits and to calm down a little. When at last Chips and I cantered into the arena we looked as cool and collected as ever, and much to the relief of my parents and our friends, we showed no sign of making the mistakes which would have been natural in the circumstances.

Sheila Baker had been pressed into service previously as an official, and found her duties consisted of collecting judges' score-sheets and taking them to the steward in charge of the marking-board. It was she, who had the first look at my marks, and came rushing towards us with the 'thumbs up' sign. I had received an almost incredible score at a time when I'd thought it only too probable we should make a real mess of the test. We were in first place with the amazing score of only 47.67 penalties, Frank Weldon on Kilbarry was on 66 penalties, followed by Diana Mason and Tramella with 79.71. Michael Naylor-

Leyland on Bright Prospect was 82.27, and Bertie Hill had picked up 192.33! I had a lead of 18.33 marks over the last season's unbeaten combination Weldon and Kilbarry. The newspapers, The Times and the Telegraph made a point of commenting on the length and unusual difficulty of the show jumping course. But Kilbarry produced a clear round, which meant that I also had to go clear to retain my lead. Chips rose to the occasion and also went clear. All would now depend on what happened on the cross-country course the next day.

Weldon was going to be trying his heart out to take the lead from me by going faster over the diverse and difficult fixed fences, and he had huge advantages with Kilbarry, who was a big, strong Thoroughbred gelding who possessed a ground-consuming fast gallop and considerable cross-country experience. He was also the current European Champion, having won at the Championships at Windsor. This was where Chips and I had competed in our very first three-day event less than a year ago.

The weather was still wet and cold and the going very deep in places. Mummy was shaking like a leaf as we went around on foot and she must have kept St Jude very occupied for the rest of the day. Despite the weather, there were lots of spectators, all agog to see if this nineteen-year-old girl from the north was going to beat the established champion.

Weldon went around very fast earning 19.5 bonus points to be deducted from his dressage penalties, a final score of 46.5. Bright Prospect managed to finish even faster with 19.8 bonus marks. Chips set off when these two were back in their stables and no doubt their riders inwardly wishing that I would fall off, refuse, go the wrong way, anything to stop me winning. But nothing like that happened. We sailed through the mud, over obstacles which Chips had never seen before and we came in with 15 bonus points, therefore winning by 13.83 points ahead of Kilbarry. My family and friends were absolutely delighted and tremendously proud of Chips' performance. I was very touched by the congratulations of perfect strangers who came up to me to say how pleased they were for me.

Returning from the on-foot presentation we were met with the vision of bottles of champagne and glasses produced magically by Sheila Baker in the back of the horsebox. We celebrated with Chips watching with interest. Champagne had never tasted so good.

I stayed on in the Cotswolds until it was time to leave for Badminton, and Chips and I became fitter than ever as a result of the long rides we took up and down the steep hills and vales. It was such different country from that at home, which is very flat, and the extra effort Chips had to make each day soon showed in the bulge of muscles rippling below his coat and his general hardness.

I turned twenty-one on the twelfth of March, but I had no time to think about this, all my efforts went into getting prepared for Badminton. In those days twenty-one for a well-brought up young lady was much 'younger' than the average twenty-one-year old in these modern times. I was an innocent in terms of men, and really only focused on getting to the top in my sport.

We arrived at Badminton as fit as any horse and rider could be. It was my first visit to these great trials, so well-known now, even to non-horsey people. Badminton House provides an impressive background to the parkland in which the trials are held, and one cannot help but feel a little in awe of the prospect of riding here for the first time. This was also the Olympic year, so the course was a tough one to test the 'probables' for the British Team, and with this extra attraction, attendance at the event was colossal.

I had never seen such crowds at any other trials. I was amazed to see the hordes of keen spectators who arrived early on dressage day. Their idea was to watch the dressage until they became bored, wandered over to the steeplechase course and then walked the four and a half miles of cross-country with their dogs, meeting friends *en route* and having a wonderful time chattering away. Most of the spectators would have had horses of their own in those days. Many were of the hunting fraternity and it was amusing to hear them pontificating with the greatest assurance and authority. This was fifty years ago, now Badminton is a spectacular, dazzling jamboree with the best shopping you could ever find - and trade stalls with every type of 'horsiana'.

Chips and I were to perform our dressage test in the afternoon. We rode out into the sunshine to do some loosening up work in the practice arena and were then called forward by the steward to go into the collecting ring. The flowers, in their brilliant white containers, had been placed around the outside of the dressage arena in line with the markers, each of which was showing a letter of the alphabet which riders and judges had to follow whilst performing and judging the test. The flowers were works of art in their own right and had been carefully watered and lovingly checked for their symmetry and perfect alignment early in the morning.

I always wanted to impress the judges right from the outset. Today's judges were Lorna Johnstone, Colonel V.D.S. Williams and Henry Wynmalen. When I saw that they had finished writing and raised their heads, I knew they were watching. I gave Chips the aids to produce beautiful half-passes at the trot to left and right going up towards them by flowing in between the flower containers. Then I showed them his extended trot with smooth transitions from collection to extension and back to collection. The bell rang. It was time to enter and begin.

First, we had to go up to the Royal Party and give a deep bow and a smile, and then turn left, past the judges, and give the aid for Chips to move into an ordinary canter down the long side and curve in well back from the arena to meet the centre line with the official in charge of opening and closing the board at A, doffing his hat in the wind. All the way up the white line to G – plenty of opportunity for the judges to see if the horse could remain dead straight, with his hind legs following exactly in line with his front ones – then to a direct halt and a salute.

We proceeded at an ordinary walk, and the judges gave their first mark out of the maximum six, turning right at C we increased the walk from ordinary to extended from the quarter marker M diagonally across the arena, treading on the centre X, and on to the far quarter marker K, and all the time the judges would be looking to see if the horse's hind legs were clearly over-tracking his front ones, and to check if he remained straight and steady. This test had a great deal of walking at the beginning, which is the hardest pace to execute well.

When we had completed the test and left the arena, Chips and I waited in the collecting ring until our marks were announced. We were thrilled to have achieved what was described in the newspapers as 'a great test' on 57.78 penalties, which took us into the lead. I could hardly believe we had beaten Tramella and Diana Mason by a huge margin of 31.68 marks. She had been the acknowledged leader in dressage for some time in the British events and had also led in the dressage in Basle. Later on, it was Kilbarry's turn in the arena and he also outdid himself. He took over the lead, displacing us by 1.56

marks to finish with 56.22 penalties. Laurie Morgan, Australia's leading rider was in third place on 73.33, and Diana Mason and Tramella were tying fourth with Michael Naylor-Leyland and Bright Prospect on 81.9. All was now dependent on how fast we could go on the next day's cross-country.

At the end of the dressage phase there was a tiny margin between Kilbarry and Chips. I needed to get my head round this situation and I went to talk to Chips, but the stables were open to the public on dressage day and people wanted to say, 'Well done'. It would have been churlish not to chat to them but as soon as I was free I set out onto the cross-country course to be alone and to look, in particular, at the Vicarage Ditch, which had a downhill approach to a yawning wide hole with very solid parallel bars set in front and behind. It was a real rider stopper. If a horse refused there a first time it would be a miracle if he or she could be persuaded to jump it having seen the depths below. Tramella did exactly that and her rider, Diana Mason wisely withdrew her before elimination. As I looked at it on the ground, I decided that it demanded a very determined approach with the last few strides full of increasing impetus. I concluded that if I brought Chips into it on the exact right stride, we would be over before he had time to have a fit.

The Coffin was a different matter. This needed a 'coiled' but forceful and determined jump in over the first rails to land downhill, one balanced stride to the ditch, jump across this 'coffin', take another stride on the upward slope, pressing the accelerator and pushing hard to reach the second set of beech rails with the balance and impetus to meet the rails perfectly. Come in too slowly and the horse would look into the ditch and refuse.

There was another intimidating fence out in open country towards the Luckington Road called the Faggot fence. Constructed of packed solid brushwood, it masked a big ditch on the landing side and a nasty drop. Once again, my answer was to come in well in hand but fast enough to clear what lay beyond. It was another fence that a horse would not jump after a first refusal. Most of the obstacles were 'island' fences, meaning that there was nothing to stop a horse running out on one side or another. They were not inviting, and one needed a horse that would listen to its rider and stay on line.

I was determined we should do well on this second day, and in due time we set off on the first phase, 17.54 miles to go. Roads and tracks gave way to the steeplechase, and round we galloped at a cracking pace to gain maximum bonus points. Straight on then through the next energy-sapping phase until we emerged at the start of the cross-country. It was the most enormous course with several really nasty fences, for in this Olympic year the Selectors were determined to test the courage and capabilities of the horses and their riders. In the five minutes I always allow before setting out on this hazardous phase, I learnt that two of the potential Olympic Team horses had been eliminated, but I didn't wait to be told where, for that knowledge would only have made me even more apprehensive, and it is the easiest thing in the world to communicate one's feelings, especially fears, to a horse.

The timekeeper called us up to the start, and off we went towards the first fence, a simple straightforward brushwood – up and over. Galloping strongly, Chips pressed on farther along the course until we reached the fateful Vicarage Ditch, the first of a series of big fences. We shot towards it, and landed safely on the far side, then it was the enormous drop fence, the Irish bank, and the water-jump where, but for Chips' inherent pony cleverness, we might have been in trouble, for he had jumped rather too short.

Fence after fence we left behind us, until at last the finish came in sight. Still going strongly, we leapt the last fence into the lake and turned to race up through the finish posts. The marks came through, and it was announced I had gained maximum bonus points for both steeplechase and cross-country. Now we knew our performance could not be bettered.

Meanwhile, Kilbarry was on the course. He, too, went around the steeplechase with maximum bonus points for speed and finished the cross-country course the same way. I had no idea what was going on while I was busy dealing with Chips, but a rumour had already started that spectators at the Vicarage Ditch, had seen him hesitate before jumping that fence and at The Lake it was being reported that Kilbarry had taken at least one distinct step backwards before jumping. If this was correct, then it constituted a refusal and twenty penalty points. The rumour grew as spectators moved about, and people gathered at the giant scoreboard on the main thoroughfare waiting to see if he had been penalised. Usually the marks go up fairly quickly but this time, very unusually, there was an extremely long wait before Kilbarry's marks were chalked in, showing no jumping penalties. In those days the television coverage of the cross-country was very sparse and what there was, was confined mainly to the fences nearest the start and finish. It was very unfortunate, to say the least, from everyone's point of view, that there was no film available to show Weldon and Kilbarry at this particular fence to prove or disprove the case. John Board, a very experienced equestrian artist and reporter, writing in *Country Life*, referred to "a distinct hesitation at the Lake".

I had to be very circumspect about this situation, at the time, and made a point of congratulating Weldon as soon as I saw him. After all, nothing could take away my pleasure in Chips and his brilliant performance and at that time I was content with my second place after the speed and endurance. I consoled myself that in any case, there would be another day and another Badminton for me, and I intended to beat Kilbarry and Weldon in the future. I was very competitive, I would always want to be first, and I would work very hard towards a win over him in 1957. But they were about to make a move against me to make sure that I never had a chance to compete with Chips again.

After settling Chips, I went up to the scoreboard to see what everyone else had done. One of the members of the Olympic Selection Committee came up to me and said bluntly that Chips was wanted for the Stockholm Olympics for Michael Naylor-Leyland to ride. He would be required at Windsor immediately for six weeks' training before Stockholm in June. I was shattered. I told him that Chips was my one and only eventer and that I did not believe he would go for a man, especially someone as tall as Michael who had also had the advantage of two horses in Badminton and had managed to get eliminated on both of them in the cross-country. Chips needed a certain type of riding and a love and understanding that no man would be capable of giving him. The Selector left me, and I was feeling utterly devastated. My parents arrived and shared my horror at this latest move of the already established leaders in the sport of eventing. Mummy and Daddy knew what battles Chips and I had had, and it was ludicrous to expect a stranger, with no personal feeling for his Olympic mount, to be able to strike up anything approaching the partnership which had been established between myself and my horse.

Worse was to come. Not long afterwards I was approached yet again by Selectors in force who in no uncertain terms told me that they had lost three of their selections for the British Team, leaving them with no possible fourth member for the Olympics. They were ruthless. Without my lending Chips, they said, the upholding of Britain's prestige in Stockholm would be in jeopardy. I felt awful, but still could not agree to this, not just for myself but also for Chips' well-being. He was more than just a horse for me. They went away for reinforcements. All this bombardment was going on whilst I was trying to prepare both Chips and myself for the finely balanced matter of the show jumping the next day which would produce the winner. The last thing I needed was this sort of pressure and upset.

A third envoy took me quietly to one side. He said he was an Equerry to the Queen and said that Her Majesty had asked specifically that I lend or sell Chips. This really did upset me. I was a staunch monarchist. I knew how keen the Queen was on horses and I could not believe that if she knew all the circumstances that she would ask this of me. I had visions of being dragged off to the tower and was dreadfully upset. I rushed to tell my parents and none of us knew what to do for the best. We would be pariahs, ostracised, although I did not think this mattered much as we did not know many competitors, we were too new to eventing and not very welcome, although the spectators and the Press for their part were very supportive and interested. Perhaps, Daddy said, as we tried to eat dinner at their hotel, it would be best to sell Chips, to make a clean break. I burst into tears, but by the end of this horrific evening I began to see there was no way out. I was going to have to sell my horse to some syndicate of anonymous money men who were committed to producing the purchase price in situations like this, and after breakfast next day we would tell the Selection Committee of our decision. I went to bed with eyes red from crying, I felt as if my heart was breaking. I knew that I would never have another Chips, he was my one true love.

Meanwhile Mr Marsh, whom I have already mentioned, who was staying in the same hotel as my parents, stopped Daddy on the stairs and said how sorry he was about the situation. He told Daddy that he personally was prepared to buy Chips, for the sum of five thousand pounds and would place him at the disposal of the Team. As part of the deal he also promised that if Chips returned from Stockholm safe and sound, then I could ride him in the following spring trials. Obviously, this appealed to me very much more than selling him to a syndicate with never a hope of having any more to do with him, so in the end we agreed to accept this most generous offer. By the time of the show jumping the next day, I was riding Chips again – but he was no longer my horse. He had been sold to the obliging Ted Marsh.

Two o'clock, and time for the parade in the main ring of all horses and riders still in the competition. I was determined not to let Chips down by doing something stupid. We both tried our hearts out and Chips produced a perfect clear round with not a sign of knocking down a fence. Now, I just had to wait and see what Weldon and Kilbarry would do. In they came and scrambled round nervously, knocking and nearly dislodging the Gate and hitting the Hogs Back so hard that it jumped up into the air only to fall straight back into the cups. But neither fence fell, and the pair emerged with no penalties and kept their lead. Once again, I made sure that I was one of the first to congratulate the winner. The Queen presented me with a silver trophy and asked a few questions about Chips which was lovely, then it was time for me to accept the good wishes of friends and strangers alike. I rode back to the stables with the awful knowledge that I might never see Chips again, and that the men would be riding him, which I could hardly bear to contemplate. Chips would wonder why I had abandoned him, and I had no way of explaining the situation to him.

The next morning, I had to hand him over to the grooms who were taking the Team horses to Windsor for training, and I watched him walking out of my life, disappearing from sight when the ramp went up and they drove out of view.

We drove home next morning with an empty horsebox and what should have been a happy homecoming was so marred by the absence of the horse who had brought me so much good luck. I busied myself at home with Ripalong but all the time I was thinking of Chips, and how he was reacting to his strange surroundings.

I kept in touch with Mr Marsh who invited me to call him Ted, which I found difficult until I got used to the idea. He had lent his horse Wild Venture to the Team, a big quality Thoroughbred gelding which he had ridden into tenth place at Badminton. This was a typically generous gesture as he knew he had neither the time nor the expertise to ride in the Olympics himself.

I was asked to go to Windsor the following week, just to explain Chips' idiosyncrasies and the way I rode him so that his new rider or riders might get the best out of him. This was the first indication that something was going wrong. Chips probably hated them as they would treat him like a machine, there to be used. No love. I arrived at Windsor and the Royal Mews where Chips and I had stayed prior to going to Turin, only to be told that he had gone lame on the fourth day. All the time I had had him he had been sound as a bell and he had done nothing at Badminton which would account for lameness, especially some days after the event. Something had happened at Windsor, but no one was going to tell me what they had been doing with him, nor who was riding him. I was upset by his appearance, his eyes looked dull, no longer bright and interested. No one would take him out of his box so that I could see this declared lameness. I returned home to tell my parents the news, and gloom descended on Mythop Road.

The next thing we knew was that Chips must be sound again, for one morning I opened the daily paper to find a photograph of him being jumped by Michael Naylor-Leyland at the Royal Windsor Show. He was entirely out of balance and literally crashing through a red wall in a show jumping competition. It clearly showed a gross misunderstanding between horse and rider as to when to take off and I was thoroughly upset all over again. The men, patently, had no idea of how he should be ridden. I telephoned Ted Marsh asking what was going on. He replied that the committee had told him that Chips was lame again and they were sending him to Ted's home at Kinver. Yet another change of scene for poor confused Chips. I telephoned Ted again as soon as Chips arrived, and Ted told me that he ran up perfectly, with no sign of lameness.

So, the Team had lied and he was not lame. They obviously couldn't handle him and used lameness as an excuse, to cover their ineptitude. Ted told me that he was going to turn him out. I suddenly realised that there might be a chance for me to buy him back when Ted told me he had no intention of riding Chips himself. He was the first decent, sensible and understanding man I had met during this whole sorry episode. I telephoned a third time, to say that I would like to discuss the situation with him, and I was immediately invited to stay with him and his wife for the weekend. Arriving at Dunsley Hall, I was made very welcome by Ted, although it was obvious that his wife hated horses and his friends. She also had a very embarrassing habit of denigrating her husband in front of any guests at any opportunity. She used a range of swear words, most of which I had never heard before, to make her point and I was horrified but had to pretend not to notice. I could not imagine what Mummy would say. No one in our house swore. I had never heard before any of the words Mrs Marsh used with such vehemence.

In the morning Ted put me on one of his many beautiful horses and we rode out into the estate for him to show me his cross-country fences. We jumped them, first one following the other, then in tandem. It was wonderful. Ted was so easy to talk to and we chatted away about all sorts of things. I liked him so much. Next morning, before I set off back to Lytham, we crossed the Kidderminster road to ride over the other side of the estate and farmland, which to my unaccustomed eyes in these matters, was vast. I commented how marvellous it must be to enjoy such a place and how lucky he was. He agreed, but said it came with a lot of responsibilities. I could see that.

The previous evening, after dinner, we had talked about Chips, who had clearly been delighted to see me again. On the morning I had arrived I had gone to the gate of his field. I called out to him and his head came up like a shot and with a loud neigh of recognition and, 'Thank God, she's come to rescue me', he set off at a canter towards me. Skidding to a halt just in time, he butted me with his head. I stroked his forehead and told him everything would be alright.

Ted seemed to understand how much I wanted Chips to be mine again and I said I would pay him the whole amount of £5,000, which was what he had paid me, if he would keep Chips safe in the field until I returned from watching the Olympic Three-Day Event in Stockholm. It was a huge amount of money to me but it was no contest between this nest egg and the return of Chips. Ted probably thought I was naïve to make this offer for the word would soon spread throughout the eventing world that this horse wouldn't go for anyone but myself. Of course, I could have offered much less, but I wanted to demonstrate to Ted my faith in Chips and that there was nothing wrong with him, as long as he was happy and properly ridden. It was the riders who had been at fault, obviously they didn't understand my wonderful horse's psyche. Ted accepted the return of his money, and said that I could come and stay any time before I left. The Goodfellows from Wick Vale had invited me to join their party for Stockholm, and at the beginning of June we all set off for Sweden from London Airport with a plane load of other supporters.

Meanwhile, Chips would stay safe in his field at the side of the house where Langley, the Head Groom, could keep an eye on him. During the next three weeks I made two journeys to see Chips and rode Ted's horses in the indoor school to improve their dressage for him. Each time Chips was delighted to see me and on my last visit I told him that the next time I was there, I would be bringing the horsebox to collect him as soon as I returned from viewing the Olympics.

That week there was a comment in one of the leading equestrian magazines on its Editorial pages: "Jim Russell told me at Bricket Wood that High and Mighty is out at grass and quite sound again. On top of this I hear that Sheila Willcox has now bought him back from Mr Marsh and hopes to have him ready for the Harewood Three-Day Event on September 20-22. This seems to be a very happy ending to an unhappy episode which rebounds to the credit of Mr Marsh and Miss Willcox, but to nobody else!"

Badminton, 1956. Chips and I jumped the fearsome drop-fence after the Vicarage Ditch.

Badminton, 1956. Jumping into the Coffin with Chips still brimful of running.

The final show-jumping phase. Chips and I landing over one of the fences during our clear round.

Chapter Eleven – Stockholm Olympics, 1956

The Team for Stockholm had been announced and consisted of Colonel Weldon and Kilbarry, Bertie Hill with Her Majesty the Queen's Countryman, and Lawrence Rook on Ted Marsh's Wild Venture. By the time we arrived on Swedish soil, the Team and Officials were all settled in at the Army stables in a huge barracks near the stadium.

The day before the three-day event was to begin, I was taken into the courtyard to watch the preliminary veterinary examination. This was great fun as I met many of my erstwhile rivals from the Turin Trials, who were once again representing their countries. They were all most surprised to see me in mufti, and wanted to know why I was not going to ride!

However, even had I been considered worthy of the honour, as a mere female I should have been barred by the existing rules governing the Olympic Trials. These allowed that only men could ride in this greatest test of all, although for a European Trial, women become eligible, as at Turin and Basle. At these Olympic Games the rules barring women from competing in the show jumping had been revoked for the first time, and it seemed possible that by 1960 those governing the three-day event might also be changed. The people who were against the inclusion of women claimed that if, during the cross-country phase if any female member of a team met with an accident, she would be more unlikely than a man to be able to continue on the way to the finish. For finish she must, or the whole team was eliminated. In the Olympic Games a team consists of three members, all of whose scores count in the final scoring, whereas in a European trial, there could be four in a team but still only the best three totals count. It is a very debatable question, but the fact remains that throughout the world's history, women have shown courage and perseverance equal to that of any man. It seems only fair to give us another opportunity to show our worth!

The horses were all passed by the panel of veterinary surgeons and returned to their boxes ready to start their great test on the next day. I was glad not to be riding some of the foreign horses over what was sure to be the most gruelling course. Some of them looked only half-fit, and others of quite the wrong type to stand up to the long test. The dressage phase was to take place in the stadium, and the day passed by without undue excitement. The Swedish Royal Family, and our own Queen and Prince Philip were present to see the British horses put up a good show, and when all the tests were finished, we stood in a fine position.

After the last British competitor made his exit, I joined the Team and their party to go on a tour of inspection of the cross-country course. It was a few miles out of Stockholm in the most beautiful scenery. The fences themselves lay mostly in the depths of thick pinewoods, where all noise was muffled by the layers and layers of pine needles, and splashes of colour greeted one from the little clusters of wild plants, and lilies-of-the-valley. It was a heavenly spot, and for once I was able to appreciate the beauties of the venue instead of ignoring my surroundings to the exclusion of all but the fences. There were some enormous obstacles, but I was relieved to find no trap fences; each one presented its own individual problem, but to an experienced horse and rider, such as one expects to find in an Olympic Team, none of them should have presented too great a difficulty. It was certainly a big course, no one could possibly deny the fact, but at this level of competition what else can be expected?

We walked on along the course and met the television interviewers at one of the fences, already siting their cameras for the next day's thrills and spills. They had a word with members of our Team, and then asked me what I thought of the course. Since then I have had plenty of time to reflect on my opinion but have changed it not in the least. It was a perfectly fair course, and the fact that one fence in particular caused much grief, was due not to the type of obstacle in itself, but to the uncontrollable weather element – an overnight shower of torrential proportions, which soaked through the top few inches of ground, and at this particular spot turned the approach into an unforeseen hazard. The course builders could be blamed in no way for the grief this fence caused; before the first rider set out on the course it looked quite innocent, and once the fact was apparent that it might become a death-trap, it was too late for anything to be done. Obviously, the fence could not be eliminated from the course, for that would mean several of the competitors suffering from a disadvantage as a result of penalties and falls already incurred, and as it was negotiated safely even at its most dangerous state the fence was not in actual fact unfair. The horses had been a long way by the time they reached this fence twenty-two, and those who were not at the peak of fitness paid the penalty.

There were enormous crowds on the cross-country course, and the British supporters had evolved a scheme on the relief system, which would provide for one of them to be present at each fence, ready to help in case ill-fortune should overtake one of our representatives. We also decided to include the Irish, Australian, and Canadian Teams in this proposed work of mercy, but agreed to remain impassively sphinx-like in the case of accidents befalling any other unfortunate. It was a good idea, and at the appropriate time I, as one of the chosen, stationed myself at the allotted fence. A horse approached, jumped over the obstacle, and thundered away into the distance. I began to look around hopefully for my relief to arrive from the previous jump so that I| could walk on to the next fence and relieve the person there, and at last she came up and I was able to move on.

For some fences the scheme worked admirably, but then, there were three or four of us at a particular jump, and apparently the same circumstances prevailed in front and behind. Our brilliant organisation had fallen to pieces, and it was left for us to carry on round the course at will, and hope to be present if anything untoward did occur. As it happened our services were not strained at all, although I did help to save one of the Canadians from missing out a fence towards the end of the course as he galloped on his way at full speed. Luckily, we were in a position to see just what was going to happen and yelled to him at the top of our voices where the next fence was – away to his left. Horse and rider slowed their pace, swung round and made for the right obstacle; eventually they finished the course, as indeed did all the members of the Canadian Team.

The many thousands of people present that day had churned up the ground until it resembled a mud bath, and by evening I was completely covered with grey slime from my calves down. I was anxious to get back to the hotel and have a bath and change, so that there would be plenty of time to prepare for a great occasion. The day before an invitation had arrived to a cocktail party on board the Royal yacht, *Britannia*, and naturally enough, I was tremendously excited at the prospect of going aboard her. There was a panic-stricken hour when word went around that hats would be *de rigeur* for the ladies, and for my part I was thrown into a state of frenzy wondering what should form my crowning glory. I hardly ever wore a hat, and although I did have a black coolie shaped one with me, the idea that it might possibly blend with the rest of my outfit never occurred to me. Soon I was deluged with offers of hats belonging to friends in the hotel, until my room began to look like a milliner's shop. I tried them all on, one by one, but I came to the conclusion that no suitable hat for me had ever been created. As a last resort, standing spick-and-span in party wear, I tried on my own black 'coolie' and to my utter amazement, the outfit was complete.

I went to the Royal yacht in all my glory, to be deflated at the sight of bare heads in plenty, so all my worry had been unnecessary. However, all was soon forgotten in the experience of being on board *Britannia*. She was a lovely vessel, shining blue and white in the evening sunshine as the guests were ushered aboard. We crossed several gangways before eventually reaching the fore-deck on which the party was being held. A giant striped awning, producing the effect of a marquee, had been placed overhead, and we all passed under its flaps to make our bows and curtseys to Her Majesty the Queen and Prince Philip, who stood just inside. The Royal couple mixed with competitors, Britishers and ships' officers alike, moving quietly from group to group, and the time passed all too swiftly. Before long we were making our way back towards the quayside and away from the *Britannia*, as she lay rocking gently in the waters of her dock.

We drove on to the stadium where already demonstrations of Swedish National Dancing were in progress, and the galaxy of colour was followed by the more subdued, but equally artistic performance of advanced dressage movements such as the corbette, levade and capriole by officers of the famous Cadre Noir Military School of France. These dressage exercises were used to advantage by cavalry officers and their mounts in the battlefields of long ago, but nowadays, they are taught to the horses to preserve a great art.

Only the show jumping phase now remained, and an expectant crowd was crushed into the stadium. The course was a long and twisty one, and most of the horses made heavy weather of it. There were only two clear rounds. Britain won the Team gold medal and the Captain, Colonel Weldon and Kilbarry won the Individual bronze medal behind a Swede and a German. It was a fitting climax to years of concentrated effort by the British Horse Society for this very event, and from being very much the 'poor sister' at her debut in the Olympic Trials in 1948, Britain now stood supreme among the world's best.

The next four days were devoted to the Grand Prix dressage, which is very advanced, and the Grand Prix show jumping, in which Pat Smythe took part – the first-time women were allowed to represent their countries as members of the Team. They were already eligible for inclusion in the advanced dressage, and Britain had two representatives in Mrs Williams and Pilgrim, and Mrs Johnstone with Rosie Dream. As an illustration of the time it takes to bring a horse to this high level of training, it is interesting to note that only three, or at the most four, horses are produced by a rider in a lifetime, which illustrates just how much work is involved. Years and years of patient teaching have passed before the animal is ready to stride into an arena for these tests. He must carry out the most intricate movements with grace and ease while his rider sits quietly, at one with his or her horse, giving no noticeable aids, yet all the time controlling and directing the symphony of movement. Advanced dressage, brilliantly executed, is a pleasure to watch, and I hoped that in time, I would be able to join the ranks of its exponents, in this ballet of equestrianism.

The show jumping was the last of the Olympic events, and the course was enormous. The speed at which some of the riders and horses took the fences was incredible. I stood in awe of the skill displayed by the German, Herr Winkler with his horse Halla, when he clinched his Individual victory with a beautiful faultless round in the afternoon while riding in great pain.

At last, it was all over, and with a final fanfare of trumpets the closing ceremony drew to its conclusion, and the Olympic flame was extinguished for another four years, when once again it would burn brightly for the 1960 Games in Rome.

During my stay in Stockholm, I met one of the directors of the greatest equestrian magazine in the world, *L'Annee Hippique* – produced in Switzerland, the delight of horse-lovers everywhere. M. Cornaz was staying in the same hotel as me, and during the week we became firm friends. I was asked to write an article for *L'Annee Hippique* on 'Feminine Impressions of Stockholm', in terms of the three-day trials. When I returned home, I dispatched the article to Switzerland. Several days later I received an ecstatic note. My family and I were so pleased with the success of my first real foray into the literary field. From time to time, little notes, written half in English, half in French, continued to arrive, and delighted us all when read over the breakfast table.

After the close of the Games, we set off on the return journey by plane. It was very warm when we left Stockholm, and as the sun shone so our spirits mirrored its warmth, and the flight was imbued with a tremendous sense of reflected glory in the triumph of our British Team. The presence of Richard Todd, the film star, as a passenger contributed even further to the atmosphere.

My parents were waiting for the Goodfellows and me at London airport, and after piling luggage into one taxi and squashing ourselves into another car, we bade farewell to our fellow enthusiasts and set off on the long journey up north.

Chapter Twelve – The Partnership Resumed

The International Horse Show took place in July, and I went as a spectator. Not that I should have been riding Chips there in any case, as there were no classes for us at White City, although there was a combined training event run at Brickett Wood in conjunction with the 'International'. This competition consisted of dressage and show jumping phases, without any cross-country. I had never yet been to Brickett Wood, as in July Chips had always been resting in between the spring and autumn trials seasons. He was roughed off after Badminton, and spent a month or two in a blissful state of luxurious laziness, with nothing to do but eat and sleep for twenty-four hours a day. In the autumn, too, he had another rest as soon as the last trials were over, which lasted until the beginning of January, when preparation of horse and rider began again.

In those days it was accepted practice that horses should have rest periods when they got fat out at grass. These days it is more common practice for them to be kept fit at least to some extent. If you consider the case of a top athlete, should they spend three months of their year lying on the sofa eating chips and ice-cream, not at all!

I arrived in London that July in seventh heaven, for Chips was mine again. All that week at White City I could scarcely conceal my elation. The Sandhurst Passing-Out Parade coincided with the show week, and my parents and I were to watch John play his part in the historic ceremonies. The weather was at its best as we watched the shining ranks of cadets marching past Princess Margaret at the saluting base. This was before Princess Margaret married and she was the most beautiful and sophisticated young woman, well-known for her witty off-the-cuff comments. The Parade was an awe-inspiring and splendid sight as the last row of senior cadets, following the Commandant on his grey horse, passed up the wide white steps and disappeared through the gateway of Old College, leaving the strains of 'Auld Lang Syne' lingering on the square – empty now, except for the junior cadets. It was a great day, and that evening at midnight the seniors all received their commissions, and became fully-fledged second-lieutenants, ready to be launched into regular army life.

The first thing I did when I got home to Mythop Road was call Ted Marsh. It was arranged that I would go with the horsebox in two days' time, stay overnight at Dunsley and then return to Lytham with Chips after lunch the following day. Chips was soon to be home again!

When I arrived at Dunsley, I found him out in the field with Crispin, and as soon as I called from the gate, he flung up his head and with a neigh of greeting galloped over to nuzzle me. I told him he would be going home to Lytham the next day, and he stood at the gate watching as Ted and I went around the corner and into the house.

The following morning, Ted had one of his fantastic horses, Blue Jeans, saddled up for me and we rode around the estate and jumped fences wherever we went. It was a far cry from my search for something safe to jump when I was training Chips at home. I told Ted that I was short on time to get Chips one hundred per cent fit for the big event of the autumn season, the Harewood Three-Day Event. This was the event which I had competed in last year and had come first in the dressage phase but had dropped to a final fourth after two mistakes due to my inexperience at cross-country. Hopefully, we had moved on and would produce a better performance. I had so much to prove particularly to the Olympic Selectors, and the riders who had sat on Chips before he was classified lame and returned to Ted. I knew that the Press and the general public had been supportive of me, but in terms of the governing powers of eventing I was definitely an outsider.

It was now the last week in June 1956, and Harewood opened with its dressage on 20th September. This meant that the twelfth week coincided with the opening of the event, whereas on my usual schedule we should have another two weeks before a big three-day event. There was also the fact that I must not rush the road work just in case the treasures at Windsor had actually managed to lame Chips there. Although when I had examined his legs with great care they were as they had always been with me, perfectly cool and sound. I also had to find out if he was still going to try for me after all the trauma of falling into the hands of men who did not understand him.

After lunch, I was out in the stables where Langley, Ted's Head Groom had brought Chips in from the field during the morning to brush his coat over, clean out his hoofs and oil them, in an effort to make him a little more presentable for his return to Lytham Hall. As I put on his bandages with the soft and comfortable gamgee tissue underneath, I told Chips that he was going home and we would then be back to our old routine. He was very fat from the paradise grass in Ted's field. I commented that he was going to have to get rid of it and become lean and fit once again. He ignored me pointedly. It was time to go.

The ramp of the horsebox was let down, and I buckled up Chips' polished headcollar, brought with me from home, and led him inside. His ears went forward as he was tied to the iron ring at one side and he peered through his windows over the cab below, looking remarkably pleased with life. The ramp went up and I stood at the driver's door and turned to say goodbye to Ted. Instead of giving me the usual peck on the cheek, he kissed me purposefully on the lips, his hands on both my shoulders. This was not a platonic kiss, and it affected me greatly. I fairly shot into the cab hardly daring to look him in the eyes and drove out of the gate, turning left to meet the Kidderminster road and travel home to Lytham.

I thought about this while driving home. Perhaps I had imagined it. I was not at all experienced in these types of circumstances, as I had only engaged in 'kissing' a little with two young men. I was an innocent in that direction. This kiss had been totally different from anything I had previously experienced. It was in the realm of grown-up experience and although I was twenty years old, I was a very young, inexperienced twenty-year-old with a sheltered upbringing, as girls of my type were in those days. I turned back to thinking about getting Chips fit, that was what was important. I tried to put it out of my mind.

Training began. Just as before the timetable hung on the wall in his stable with a pencil dangling beside it. Chips was clearly delighted to be back in his comfortable loosebox and with me in attendance, and soon we were out on the roads, going further each week. People would wave at us as we trotted along Clifton Street in Lytham, or through the Square in St Annes. I had grown up here and I felt as if I belonged.

This period also marked my first opportunity to judge dressage tests proper, and I traveled up to Edinburgh to act as co-judge at the Pony Club Area Championships at Dreghorn. It was strange to sit in the judges' tent, and watch the tests carried out from this new angle, but it helped me enormously to realise just how much a judge can view from his or her viewpoint, and how difficult it is to be sure of exact centres on the markers at which the movements in these tests are carried out, or transitions made from pace to pace. I had previously judged at local horse club events, but this was my first chance to try my hand away from home, and I enjoyed the experience immensely.

The pace at which I had to get Chips fit soon resulted in Ripalong's work being neglected. My parents laid down the ultimatum that Ripalong must go, as it was fair neither to the horse nor myself to carry on in the existing circumstances. Rip was entered for the next Leicester sale, and he was eventually sold, leaving me to carry on the lone battle of bringing Chips to fitness.

Once Chips had slimmed down and his legs were getting hard, we traveled round the country to compete in Working Hunter classes, in which the horse is judged on jumping prowess over rustic show jumps in the ring, and also on conformation, action and movement. We also competed in straightforward show jumping classes to encourage him to make an effort to produce clear rounds and not associate it just as the occupation of the last day of the three-day event when he might be sore or tired and likely to hit a fence. I tried to educate him that although the fences fell down if he hit them, this would not please me and there would be no sugar nor praise. He regained his old enthusiasm, and at the Ormskirk Show excelled himself by winning both the Grade C Jumping, Ladies Jumping and then the Foxhunter class. It was good practice and it put some well-needed money in my pocket. Although in pony books I might have been called a 'pot-hunter'! We went to other agricultural shows where he was equally consistent, and was winning with clear rounds, and then we reached the inevitable stage when we needed some cross-country practice.

I traveled to Dunsley wondering if I was doing the right thing, and also with the thought that perhaps I had imagined it all. When I arrived, Ted was still at work at the sausage factory and had left a message for me to settle Chips into his loosebox across the road, as the boxes next to the house were all occupied by the hunters being prepared for the approaching season.

I drove the horsebox over to the stables on the other side of the road. There was a herd of cows standing in the field by the gate as I turned in and unloaded him. They were making a real racket mooing loudly, complaining that it was time for them to go into their parlour and be milked, and next to their parlour were several other purely functional farm buildings. The red brick stables were set apart from these, they were warm and welcoming, and comprised several looseboxes with a fodder room, and other store rooms to the side. Further on was the Estate Office, where I was to learn that Tristram, Ted's Personal Assistant and confidant worked, along with his long-time and much valued Private Secretary, Miss Hodnett. Chips was soon settled comfortably into this new hotel where he sensibly deigned to make friends through the bars with his neighbours on either side before turning to his hay and inspecting his manger. He was housed in a line of the best hunters in the country. I wonder what they had to say to each other.

I heard a car come into the yard and the next minute in through the outer door came Ted, apologising for not being there when I arrived. He gave me a normal peck on the cheek and said we should go over to the house for tea. The perfect host, he ushered me across the road, collected my luggage from the porch and stowed it in the hall whilst a tray of tea was requested and produced from the kitchens for us in the morning room. We chatted away as if nothing had happened. His wife was nowhere to be seen, and from my previous visit I thought it better not to ask where she was. I knew they had two children, a son and a daughter. I had mentioned this to Mummy after my first visit and she had reacted in the same way as Chips did when he was grazing in the field and heard something interesting. Up would shoot his head, and he would be all attention. I could almost hear the thought leap into her head, 'Good, perhaps this will be the one for her'. His children were older than me. The way Ted had intervened at the Badminton Hotel and offered to buy Chips at that dreadful time, had made a big impression on both my parents and having digested this piece of information that there was what must be an eligible son, Mummy was more than happy for me to go to Dunsley. Nobody could say that Ted didn't know what he was doing when dealing with people!

Tony, the elder was twenty-five years old to my twenty and current Hill Climb Motor Champion. He was a brilliant mechanic and whiz with engines and presently developing a remote-control miniature boat with his like-minded friend, Duncan Hollingsworth. Judy, Ted's daughter, married Duncan in 1959 and they settled to a new life in Beech Tree Farm and then began to concentrate on retaining the purity of the Dartmoor breed on their own land. She showed ponies in hand very successfully, then kept her own stallion to serve the mares, and later on bought a top stallion who also brought in visiting mares. I met both Tony and Judy that evening, and the next morning when I was waiting for Ted to return from his office work so that we could jump the cross-country fences, it was obvious that poor Tony had been press-ganged into taking me with him to watch the small boat being controlled from a handset. It is everyday stuff now, but in those days, it was a miracle. I remember thinking how different was the son compared to his father. Tony was very taciturn and seemed ill-at-ease with me as a female in tow. Perhaps he knew his father too well and understood Ted's intentions.

At last, Ted and I rode out across the fields towards the cross-country fences and having skirted them so that Chips would not know what was next, but to ensure that I knew what we were about to jump, I stood as if at the start of a competition and Ted counted me down. Chips and I shot off towards the first fence and we sailed over that and negotiated all the others without a hint of non-cooperation. This was the first time Chips had seen cross-country fences since being at Windsor with the Olympic men and I had not known how he would react. He seemed OK and that was a huge relief. Then it was Ted's turn to jump and it was tremendous to share the same interest with someone and in such amazing surroundings. I wanted to know about his life and he told me that his Marsh and Baxter factory was in Calne, where he worked hard, and that he had a wonderful house in Anglesey and a hunting box in Ireland, both of which he would show me one day. I was at a loss to know how to respond to this.

I unpacked my suitcases after tea in a lovely large bedroom overlooking the front of the house, then having taken a bath and dressed in one of my pretty frocks from Mummy's shop, I went downstairs to the drawing room for pre-dinner drinks. As usual I had my bitter lemon with ice.

After dinner I apologised and announced I had to stick to Chips' timetable and give him his last feed at nine o'clock. Ted said he would go with me across the road. Donning coats, off we went into the night. I fed Chips and checked that he was alright and then Ted said he must go into his office and once inside he sorted out some papers at his desk whilst I looked around and then he turned to me.

"You must know that I am very fond of you."

I was not sure how to respond to this. He walked round the desk, stood looking at me with his brown eyes and then took me into his arms and kissed me. It seemed the most natural thing in the world. It was a mixture of urgency and sweetness. I felt sensations I had never had before. Where I had hated the tongue of my earliest date in my unsuspecting mouth, this one I liked and responded. The feeling of desire rose up again, and I kissed him back. I could feel my heart thudding and I experienced some very strange flutterings. I broke away in sheer self-defence and looked at him.

"I'm sorry," he said

"No, you're not," I responded.

He grinned at me boyishly. We moved together again and continued kissing. This was the beginning of what was probably the defining relationship of my life.

At the time, as overwhelming as it was, I had other things to think about - Chips and my competitive career. I returned to Lytham trying to push it all to the back of my mind. The opening one-day event of the season run by the Royal Army Veterinary Corps was approaching and in early September we set off to stay again with Mrs Edlin at Thurnby. She was the woman who had bought our Arabian stallion Algayam all those years ago.

We drove straight to the ground to give Chips his usual first sight of the event and to do a little dressage and remind him what the pair of us would be doing on the next day. The Allhusens were already there and Derek would be riding his six-year-old mare, Laurien, a fast-rising star. The three Willcoxes and Derek with his wife, Claude, had met on the circuit in the spring, and because we were all strangers to the established eventers, had soon become firm friends. At this event, unusually, there was only one class, so we were up against Derek on Laurien and Ted competing on Blue Jeans. I walked the course alone, so I could concentrate properly. Whilst the fences were not high, it was going to be no sinecure for the going was deep. This would make it tough for everyone.

The next morning Chips produced a first-class dressage test. It was his return to eventing after the debacle at Windsor with the Olympic men, and I didn't know how he was going to react. In the show jumping he horrified me by refusing at a double and knocking down one fence, but the going was so bad that only one horse managed to go clear. We had 129 penalties, Blue Jeans and Ted were second on 188, and Derek third on 189.

I was getting Chips warmed up for the cross-country and then there was long delay while the army was fishing two souls out of a ditch and by the time, we shot off through the start Chips was feeling like he didn't want to go. He was zig-zagging, his usual evasive manoeuvre and I changed my whip from right to left hand and gave him a crack on his left shoulder. He promptly went right. I responded with another sharp crack on his right shoulder. This continued until we got to the first post-and-rails, which he grudgingly jumped. Then we were heading down a slope to a set of parallel bars set over a very deep and wide wet ditch. The take-off was very slippery. Under normal circumstances, I would have collected him a little six or seven strides out, to make sure we were on the exact right stride on take-off but in his present awkward mood any sort of reduction in pace would give him an excuse to stop, so we galloped into the jump. Someone was filming this performance and when I saw it, I realised that we had jumped from a virtual standstill. Then I got serious and drove Chips on relentlessly and in the end, we had the fastest round of the day and ran out easy winners with a lead of 69.2 marks over Laurien, whilst Ted was third 33 marks behind.

I pondered Chips behaviour as I washed him down, dried him off and completed my routine of making him safe and comfortable. I cheered him up with pats and praise and sugar lumps. He must have had a terrible time at Windsor to make such an effort to move out of range of the fences and there was still some residual resistance in his behaviour, particularly in show jumping when it was part of a one-day event. It was just eleven more days to the big three-day event at Harewood and I couldn't be sure how Chips would go. We were going to need more of St Jude's blessing and assistance and Mummy would intercede for me.

Chapter Thirteen – Harewood, 1956

Mid-September, and Chips once more walked up the ramp into his horsebox at Lytham for the journey over the Pennine Way into Yorkshire. My parents and I were staying at a hotel in Harrogate and John Holt had volunteered to come along and act as groom. There was always a tremendously friendly atmosphere at these northern trials, and the organisers spared no effort to provide every facility and help for the competitors. Those southerners who cringed with horror at the thought of venturing farther north than a line drawn from Birmingham to the Wash, believed that we still wore woad and ate fish and chips out of newspaper, should have come to Harewood and sampled a taste of our hospitality!

The dressage tests usually began on a Thursday, and on the day before, all the competitors were collected together in a marquee or hall and briefed. Maps of the course were issued, any relevant explanations were made, and questions were answered by the Director of the Trials and his committee. After this briefing, which was usually about half past ten in the morning, we all piled into Land Rovers and played follow-my-leader round the phases A and C, the roads and tracks, and walk round the steeplechase course. Energy was restored by a break for lunch in the members' marquee, and then we set off in good heart to walk the cross-country course. This was the first-time competitors saw the course, while the horses never see it until they are actually competing. But once the official walk-round was over, we are then at liberty to go over the course and decide, uninterruptedly, how to jump the various obstacles.

My parents were nearly always brave enough to follow in our tracks and see for themselves the horrors which awaited Chips and me, but for some unknown reason this particular year the Harewood course stretched interminably onwards and the store of my father's energy drained to its last drop. His pace slowed to a mere crawl, and when at last he caught sight of a litter-bin, he gasped to my mother, 'Put me in that bin – I'm bound to be collected in due course!'

Colonel Weldon and Kilbarry were not to compete, and I cursed Nasser in Egypt. Due to the Suez Canal crisis Weldon's regiment was on seventy-two hours standby notice. He was there as a spectator with his father and son. I was bitterly disappointed as more than anything I wanted to beat Weldon and Kilbarry again. John Oram was there with two horses, Michael Naylor-Leyland was also competing, and our friend Derek Allhusen on Laurien, and also Jack Scott on Major. There were no competitors from abroad for they were busy with their European events. The Australians had gone home, although Laurie Morgan had left his horse, Gold Ross, in England due to the tiresome quarantine process and David Naylor-Leyland was to ride it. It was rumoured that Laurie was going to sell up in Australia and move permanently to England. Of the initial 28 horse and rider combinations that had been entered only 15 were to start.

Speed and endurance day dawned bright and clear; it was also hot – too hot for Chips' liking. He was a horse who seemed to feel much more energetic in cooler weather. In warm weather he felt no urge to strain himself more than absolutely necessary. I knew that in the circumstances the idea of hurrying along for miles and miles, just to satisfy the whim of a capricious female, would hold no great appeal for him. But I had a good talk to him before we set out, and told him just how fast I intended him to go. I could do no more than hope for the best and ride him with every ounce of strength and determination I possessed. I only hoped that his shortened training would be enough.

The course-builders had ensured that there were time-consuming easier alternatives so that the younger horses might lose time by taking the longer routes but by so doing would not be frightened or confused by too difficult a fence early in their career. Another clever move was that there was a fence in the big lake that was not flagged so any fall there would not be penalised. However, it would waste a great deal of time if the horse refused and even more if horse or rider fell, it was a conundrum. We had to enter the lake before this 'hazard' obstacle and the next numbered fence was some 50 yards away in a straight line through the water and involved jumping up and out on to the bank and off immediately away over a solid tree trunk. If one wished to avoid the 'hazard' jump in the water, you would pay a forfeit having to wade out into the deeper waters of the lake. I spent some time considering this and then decided that we would risk the 'hazard' fence.

The veterinary inspection was held, as usual, at six o'clock and Chips passed fit and well. Amongst the crowd was Victor Sassoon, a world-famous figure and multimillionaire, with racing interests and investments all around the globe. He talked to me for some time asking all about eventing, and about Chips, and things in general. He took photographs of me without me realising what he was doing, and weeks later sent me copies with a personal letter from his home at Nassau in the Bahamas.

The next day a soft white mist heralded a beautiful dressage day. For the first few competitors, visibility in the arena was limited to its length. A new system for displaying marks had been introduced. The three judges gave their scores individually by pressing their chosen marks which then flashed on outside their tent. It meant that there was no conferring between the judges and the officials would not be able to 'fix' the marks.

Chips outdid himself and was showing off, and he was awarded the best score of the day, 57 penalty points. Our nearest rival was Penny Moreton from Ireland on Korbous on 73.33, and John Oram in third and fourth position with Trident on 95.1 and Copperplate on 105.90. Michael Naylor-Leyland occupied fifth position with Laurie Morgan's horse Gold Ross on 119.23. So, we were leading by 23 points.

On cross-country day Chips was led up to the collecting ring and stood there conserving his energy as I took the saddle and 'weighed-out'. There is a minimum weight to be carried for the second day's tests, and while the men carry 11 stone and 11 lbs, women carry just 11 stone; but before you say the men must start under a disadvantage remember how very much larger, generally speaking, are the horses ridden by men, and also the fact that the men are so much heavier than the women to start with, and probably have to put up no dead weight at all.

In preparation for the cross-country I folded up Daddy's large handkerchief into a triangle and sewed two sides of it on the inside front of my number. Into this pocket went my glucose tablets. At last the steward signalled five minutes before it was Chips' and my turn to pass the posts. I made a final check of his saddlery and then jumped up to take my place under the starter's flag. Down came his arm, and off we went at a strong trot on the first phase. The roads and tracks at Harewood were the most difficult of all the events, for there were no parts where one could relax while trotting and cantering along, as at

Badminton or Windsor. At Harewood our way lay over uneven ground, and twisted along densely wooded plantation paths, which made doubly difficult the rider's task of recognising the points at which to take a time-check. This was done generally to make sure of reaching the end of the roads and tracks phases with time to spare in which to recover a little breath before the faster phases. However, I managed to keep to our schedule, by checking the scribbled figures written on a piece of paper in my breeches' pocket. We emerged at the finish of phase A, and soon set out round the steeplechase course. This was always just like the ordinary racecourse one, although our track was only temporary so there were no legitimate railings, and our way was marked with roped posts and turning flags. The fences were of birch and were all similar, except for one, the Open Ditch, which we jumped twice.

Chips was superb over this phase and took each fence in his stride. It was the most wonderful sensation. We thundered towards the fences one by one, taking off – it seemed – yards away from the obstacle, flying gracefully through the air, then landing lightly, to gallop off along the track until there were no more fences and only the monotony of the roads and tracks for the next half hour. I gave him time to regain his breath as we started on phase C, by slowing to a walk for several hundred yards, and then on we went again, trotting and cantering, keeping strictly to our scheduled programme. Chips' groom and various friends waited with cool water to sponge him down in the five minutes I had to spare, and then we were off on the cross-country phase. The first few fences were easy, and I knew immediately that Chips was going to go well. I talked to him the whole way around, soothing him or urging him on as occasion demanded, keeping up the same smooth pace whether a jump loomed ahead or simply the green sward between obstacles. As the end of the course came in sight, he was feeling tired, but with a final effort we passed the finishing post and set off on the mile-long run in. Chips was most annoyed at this further demand on his resources, for the finish of the cross-country phase coincided with the start of the whole thing, and having returned there he not unnaturally believed his job over. However, he gave in with good grace, and in no time, the speed and endurance was over for another year. Never had Chips pulled up quite as tired after a second day, but I knew his performance was miraculous in view of his hurried preparations, and after a good rubdown, cooling leg-bandages, and food and water, he was left for the night to rest his aching limbs.

That same evening the Harewood Ball was held in the Majestic Hotel at Harrogate. Most of the competitors, judges and officials were present, and it was a most enjoyable occasion, with dining, dancing and chatting away into the small hours of the morning. Then all was finished, and we returned to our hotels to take advantage of what little remaining time there was before presenting our horses at the veterinary inspection the following morning.

Chips was passed by the vets with no difficulty, for his night's rest worked wonders and he appeared fitter than ever. It often occurred to me how very much more amusing it would be to bring out the riders for inspection on the same morning, I was certainly never quite sound for the last phase, and never failed to crawl out of bed uttering groans of agony as my stiffened muscles were brought into use again. The Princess Royal and Prince Philip came down from Harewood House to watch the examinations, and the Prince talked to me for a few minutes before Chips' number was called. The Royal party went into the stables' canteen for morning coffee while competitors and their friends were still there, and this was typical of the complete and utter informality which was so pleasing a feature of Royal attendance at the trials. Actually, the Harewood catering facilities by the stables were first-class, and most of us competitors used them in preference to the members' marquee up by the main arena. There was even a television installed for the grooms, for their entertainment in the evenings, and the annual presence of the same staff ensured the usual cheerful service and kindly atmosphere.

The Duke of Edinburgh also watched the show jumping, and as we filed past the Royal Box on the parade, it was 'eyes-left' and a bow or salute from each rider still left in the field. The jumping started, and eventually it was time for Chips and me. We were in the brilliant position of having eight fences in hand, the equivalent of eighty marks, but Chips was determined to complete the trials without a jumping penalty. Going smoothly and effortlessly round the course, he came out of the ring with a clear round. It only remained for us to lead in the prize-winners and receive our awards. Prince Philip made the presentations, and was most amused when not one, but three trophies were passed to him for Chips and me. He laughingly decided to hand me one as a token offering, then clipped the first rosette on to Chips' bridle.

Harewood was over for another year, but still there remained the cocktail party in the evening at Harewood House, so there was no time to spare in our rush back to Harrogate, to change into party attire. I was nearly frantic as we eventually arrived back at the main gates, only to meet a flow of outgoing traffic. Our progress up to the House was maddeningly slow, and I was sure the Willcox family would be in disgrace for arriving late. However, all was well, for to my relief everyone else was obviously suffering in the same way, and we were actually one of the first. The Princess Royal, and the Earl and Countess of Harewood joined Prince Philip in moving among the company, and towards the end of the party an official came over to say the Duke was coming to talk to me.

Next moment I found myself answering his questions about Chips, the course and dressage in general, to the vast amusement of our small group – of which my mother was a member. He gave us his impressions of the intricacies of dressage accompanied by actions and reduced us all to a state of hilarity. By this time all the other guests were taking their leave of the Princess Royal, so in no time, I too, was joining them on the steps of the house, and with my parents drove away from Harewood and its memories.

Unlike the spring season, the three-day trials of the autumn do not provide a grand finale, and Harewood is followed by various one-day meetings all over the country. After this triumph at Harewood, Chips was given a few days' gentle exercise, and then again, we were in full training for the coming events. We competed at the Warwickshire Wellesbourne Trials, and Chips continued in winning vein with a first in the open section for the second year in succession. At Wellesbourne, the cross-country course began with a long run to the first fence, which was in a hedge lining the drive up to a farm-house. As Chips and I thundered towards it from the start, a horse-trailer was being driven merrily down from the direction of the house and I could see in an instant that we should both converge by the first fence. I was furious and shouted at the top of my voice to attract the driver's attention. Luckily my panic-stricken yells had some effect, and to my relief the trailer ground to a stop as Chips and I reached the path, to clatter across and take the fence in our stride. Chips put the rest of the course behind us with no difficulty, but for those first two hundred yards I had been really worried, and Chips must have thought he was carrying some devilish creature from outer space.

We had been invited to take part in the Personalities Parade at the Horse of the Year Show the following week, and accordingly arrived at Harringay Stadium for rehearsals the day before the Show opened. I had never been there before and was most impressed with the way in which everything was organised to the last detail. Besides Chips and me, there were Arabs, pit-ponies, a polo pony, two steeplechasers, and various others representing their own particular breed or sport, and the final entrant into the arena was the famous show jumping horse, Foxhunter, led by his old groom, George. Those in charge of the animals were to attend a rehearsal on 'Shank's pony' first of all, and we were all given our order of entry. I found myself to be the last but one, just in front of Foxhunter's George, and eventually it was my turn to caper round the arena trying to simulate Chips' grace on my own two feet – a task made doubly difficult by the fact that as yet I had not changed out of mufti, and the strain of careering about in the soft peat underfoot, balancing precariously on high heels, nearly finished me altogether.

Later on, the performance was repeated, but this time with the horses, and I must say there was a great improvement as far as I was concerned. It was really exciting, and as Marjorie would have said 'a bit of alright'. The band struck up with the effect of lifting Chips to even greater efforts. The glaring lights and noise of the indoor stadium made it even more interesting.

Riding back to the horsebox, I glanced at the caravans and recognised and waved to one or two of the show jumpers there to compete from the north. Here were the people my mother had cited as the reason for not wanting me to continue as a show jumper. I had to acknowledge that there were riotous parties going on after the late night finishes of the jumping competitions. It was straight out of Jilly Cooper's novel *Riders* with Rupert Campbell-Black and Billy Lloyd-Foxe. Although in retrospect such high jinks amongst young riders was not as sinister as the stealthy seduction techniques of old men dressed up as respectable, stolid citizens.

We gave this performance every afternoon and evening, and Chips excelled himself. As day succeeded day, his individual show improved more and more, until we were incorporating the 'passage'

– one of the more spectacular dressage movements – in the sequence. I had never taught this to him, but one evening before entering the arena, he had become rather excited, and had begun to 'passage' on his own initiative. I needed no encouragement to take advantage of this accident, and luckily Chips produced it whenever I asked for it.

On the Wednesday the Queen and Prince Philip were present at the evening performance, and as usual we were to parade as personalities. Chips was obviously not intending to let excitement get the better of him as a result of the presence of Royalty. Perhaps he now considered himself accustomed to their gaze! As we emerged from the tunnel leading into the arena itself, he calmly took his place between the two trumpeters and stood like a rock as the spotlights played upon us and the commentator said a few words as introduction. Then, to the strains of 'She's a Lassie from Lancashire', we moved forward to give our show, and came to a halt with a bow in front of the Royal Box. There was always a tremendous air of excitement during these evening performances, and both Chips and I thoroughly enjoyed the parade for the whole period of the show. I was staying just outside London, at a country-house hotel, and Chips was stabled nearby, so each day he would be led into the horsebox and driven over to Harringay. Between the afternoon and evening parades I changed out of riding clothes and wandered about the stadium meeting and talking to friends or watching the various competitions.

One particular afternoon, with the time for getting into riding-kit approaching, I walked to the park where I had left the car with all my clothes locked inside. It was a Vauxhall, with self-locking doors, although the driver's door would open with a key. Nonchalantly, I put my hand in my pocket, but when I found nothing there, I began to panic. A further frantic search proved equally fruitless, and I was forced to the disturbing conclusion that the key must be lying in the pocket of my riding-jacket, which lay tantalisingly out of reach on the back seat of the car. I went in search of the carpark attendant and told him the sad story, so he in turn found an AA man, who brought along a board of keys in the hope that one of them might fit the lock. Again, we had no luck, so then with a policeman's help, the two of them settled down to work with a steel ruler and rivalled any professional breaker-in with their skill. At last there was a click, and the latch holding the side window slid back, in a trice the lock was slipped and the door opened.

Time had been running short, so with hurried thanks I gathered up my kit and rushed back to the stadium to change and take part in the parade. Later on, I returned to the car – now open – and with time to spare. I began to look for the missing key. But still I could not find it, and although I was now in the car, I had no means of driving it away that evening. Helpful suggestions of switching-on with a hairgrip sounded fine in theory, but they certainly don't always prove as easy in practice, and but for the brainwave of a friend, I should probably still be sitting in the Harringay carpark. When all else had failed, my friend had the brilliant idea of finding a Vauxhall garage and buying another key, so off we set in search of an agent. We struck lucky straight away and found a key with the ignition number corresponding to that on my dashboard. The mere act of switching on the engine gave me greater satisfaction than I could have believed possible.

Harringay, however, did not consist only as a parade-ground for us, for on the Friday Chips and I competed in the combined training competition. This event, dressage and show jumping, took place in the outdoor stadium, and there was a host of entries. We all performed the dressage test one by one, and then jumped over a course of show jumps set in a very twisty design. Chips led after the dressage and did a clear round of show jumping, so in the evening we appeared, not only as a 'Personality' in the floodlit arena, but also as winners of the combined training, and received our rosette and trophy. As soon as the parade was finished, Chips was sent off back to his stable with my father who was to see that he would be made comfortable for the night. Mummy and I rushed to the car to drive from Harringay along the crowded London highways and out onto the road to Aldershot, where we were staying overnight in a hotel.

The next day was the army one-day trials at Tweseldown some miles away, and I had yet to walk round the cross-country course there before Chips arrived. Early in the morning we went to the meeting-place, collected my number cloths from the secretary, made sure of the scheduled time for Chips and me to do our dressage test. Eventually we found our weary way around the cross-country phase on foot, and learned the show jumping course. Meanwhile, my father had arrived driving the horsebox, and I saddled up Chips to do some loosening-up exercises and preparations for the dressage. Kilbarry and Colonel Weldon were there. As Chips and I had a lower number, we would be doing our test before them, and I had no idea how good we would have to be to beat them.

Chips and I trotted off, and in due time I finished what little preliminary work he needed before a test, and rode up to collect my cap and have Chips polished up before his grand entrance. To my horror, Walter was nowhere to be seen, and neither my parents nor any of our friends had had sight nor sign of him. Couriers were despatched to north, south, east and west in search of the missing body, while I tried on caps of varying sizes, belonging to competitor friends.

Suddenly I gave a shout for there was Walter calmly watching the proceedings from the side of the arena, utterly oblivious to the uproar his absence was causing. I rushed over to him, and pressing my own cap over my ears, I jumped on Chips, and next minute was being ushered in to do the dressage test. In spite of everything, Chips went well, and sure enough, after everyone had completed this first phase, and we all gathered round the blackboards bearing the marks and current placings, Chips and I led the field. The show jumping course seemed higher and more difficult than one finds as a general rule in the trials, and Chips increased our lead still further by producing the only clear round. Short of a fall on the cross-country, or refusals, we were 'home and dried' but Chips galloped round in great heart, to be an easy winner.

We had no time to rest on our laurels, though, for the evening shadows were already beginning to lengthen, and we had to be back at Harringay for eight o'clock to become Personalities for the last time. It was a dreadful journey back to London, for it seemed as if half Britain, and certainly all the southerners, were going our way. As we finally drew up with the horsebox by the stadium all the other parade horses were standing ready for their entry, and we had a tremendous rush to bring out Chips again and take our place as the band struck up what we had come to consider 'our tune'. The announcer told the crowd that I had only just managed to return to Harringay in time to parade before them. He explained that we had been competing at Tweseldown and had beaten the great Kilbarry. The crowd erupted, and I had to blink back the odd tear. What a week it had been!

It was much too far for us to return home before the end of the season trials, which took place at Chatsworth the following Thursday, so we were to stay at Dunsley, Ted Marsh's place. With a stroke of wicked genius, he had suggested this to Mummy and Daddy and he had also invited them to lunch as a break on their way home in the car. You can imagine how much my parents had been looking forward to seeing Dunsley of which I had told them so much. I would be staying there five nights.

We arrived, and lunch was a great success. There was no sign of his wife and Ted was an attentive host. He certainly knew how to lay on the charm. Mummy enjoyed the wonderful food and was impressed with the grand setting and comfortable ambience. After lunch Ted took Daddy out to show him his gun dogs, for Daddy was a good shot and had a gun in a little rough shoot near the Lake District. He was very interested in Ted's big shoot with its properly organised parties. They all seemed to get on well together. Then my unsuspecting parents drove off, heading for home, and left me there unchaperoned.

That evening Phil, Ted's wife, had appeared for Sunday's light supper and had given a loud sniff as Ted again volunteered to escort me over the road when it was time for me to give Chips his nine o'clock feed. In my youthful innocence I put this down to her being disagreeable, rather than understanding that she knew her husband too well.

He escorted me across the road and went straight into his office, and the kissing started immediately. This time there was a greater sense of urgency about it. Our coats came off and I felt a hot rush of fire in my pelvic area. We were very close, and his hands were caressing my back and slipped down to my bottom and pressed me close to him. I could feel how aroused he was and momentarily thought of Mummy and what she would have thought of this. Then I lost myself in feelings of longing and began to move my own hands and use my tongue. Suddenly, Ted gave a cry and shot backwards. In my innocence, I wondered what I had done wrong. He pulled out his handkerchief and opened his fly buttons to reveal an erection on the point of explosion. I had never seen this before and was fascinated. He encircled his penis with the handkerchief and came into it. Like a child, I was highly entertained with these strange antics. He recovered himself and stowed his handkerchief back into his pocket. He held me quietly for a few minutes, looked at me searchingly and then stroked my face with his fingers, tracing my lips. My natural reaction was to open my mouth and suck on his finger. This seemed to set him off again. Then he pulled himself together and suggested that we go back to the house.

I was amazed at the way he returned to his previous behaviour, exhibiting casual and polite attention. I was so innocent, and knew nothing of the wiles of men and their ability to seduce young women. I was at a stage when I was ripe to be initiated into the wonderful and exciting world of sex.

The next four days were a delight. I roamed with Chips over the estate, sometimes accompanied by Major Russell, Ted's trainer, whilst doing my two and a half hour's work. We did not need much dressage practice, but there was an arena set out in the flat paddock behind the house stables. When Ted returned from his work we would ride out on his horses, Blue Jeans for me and Leprechaun for him, and there was always something to talk about. Every evening at nine o'clock we would go over to the stables across the road and he continued to initiate me into the preliminaries of love-making.

On Friday morning, we left to go to Chatsworth House. Ted was also taking two of his competition horses. This was the first time that the Duke and Duchess of Devonshire had held a one-day event and I was amazed at the sheer size of their stately home. It was truly gigantic. I was to spend the night with the Head Gardener and his wife in their cottage. They were very welcoming, and I made new friends.

The cross-country terrain was half on the level ground where the dressage and show jumping arenas lay ready for us. The middle half of the course from Fence 6 took us up a steeply rising escarpment which we had to climb until we were near Jubilee Rock and then down we came, jumping a series of alarming drop fences, some into space. Before the ground levelled out totally the course made a sharp left hand turn over a high hump which hid from view, until the last two strides, a very daunting fence into the Ice Pond. The pond used to provide ice for the big house in years gone by. This year, it was to be a feature and had been filled with water. It looked like a miniature lake to the horses.

Then the course continued over a post-and-rails in the middle of the pond and over several more obstacles before meeting Mary's Bower, a four feet six inches deep dry circular moat around a small central island with a bower perched on top. I was told that this was where Mary, Queen of Scots, used to sit and ponder in the sixteenth century whilst Elizabeth the First (Anne Boleyn's daughter) was deciding what to do with her. Towards the end of the course we galloped alongside a wide and beautiful river, the Derwent, with its brightly polished grey stones twinkling on its bed. It was an enchanting setting for a horse trials.

After the dressage we stood 43 marks ahead of the second-placed Penny Molteno on Bandoola. In the show jumping we went clear and drew ahead, now leading by 63 marks. I had been a little worried as the show jumps looked flimsy, but this time Chips didn't come close to knocking any poles. He literally flew around the cross-country but then coming downhill, over the nasty drop fence we turned left over the hump and almost collided with the rails into the Ice Pond. I turned him round, quick as lightening, and rode towards it again and he sailed over, and then we continued to storm around the course. We gained maximum bonus points for a quick time. Our win was convincing, and it was sad to leave, saying good-bye to the Allhusens and Ted. There were no more trials until March 1957.

In December all the trials people assembled in the Russell Hotel for the Horse Trials Annual Meeting. There was a discussion of the new rules. Many other competitors were present and on meeting again we exchanged news and views. The conference opened, and we learnt eventually that the new ruling reduced the influence of the dressage phase on the total marks to one-third of one and two-day trials, and to a half of three-day trials, thereby telescoping the margin between first and last considerably, and rendering the competition much more 'open'. No longer would it be possible for anyone to emerge from the first phase in an almost unassailable position, and even the cross-country section's marking system was revised, for bonus marks for completing the course in less than the time allowed were abolished utterly in one and two-day trials. In their place a time limit was to be set to make it almost impossible to finish in the set time. So, it would be most unlikely that one could emerge without penalty marks. I decided to fit a jet-propelled engine on to Chips for the next season, for without such aid I felt we should be lucky ever to stand in the winner's enclosure again!

Horse and Hound awarded the 'Horse of the Year' in ten various categories. Chips and I won 'most successful in the field of combined training'. I was also awarded the British Horse Society's Diploma of Honour. I was living the dream and in my youthful state I could envisage nothing but a continued run of victory, hard work and good luck.

Ted invited me once again to spend time at Dunsley, to go hunting with him on his horses. He had spoken to me often since the five days I was there before Chatsworth and was saying how much he missed and wanted me. During that time my thoughts had strayed to him many times and I argued with myself about the age gap and how it was possible for me to have fallen in love with him so quickly and devastatingly. I had always imagined that in time I would fall for someone a few years older than myself, probably with the same interests, and most certainly to a man who wanted the same lifestyle to which I was becoming accustomed. I had tried to tell myself that my feelings for Ted were only those of a young girl who was flattered by the attention of a man twenty-six years older than herself. I thought that these feelings would pass.

The other problem was that he was married although he and his wife lived their lives separately by mutual agreement. The eventing people viewed him as a charming and gentle man with a dreadful wife. I reasoned with myself that most men married under the same circumstances would look for love and sex elsewhere. Ultimately, someone else would come along and they would divorce and remarry.

Ted went to extraordinary lengths to keep our budding relationship hidden. I found this amusing, rather than sinister, and teased him about it. I had fallen for a man who hid behind a mask of respectability a pillar of local society. He was a Justice of the Peace, chairman of the Farmers' Union, country gentleman. I found it fascinating that he was such a gentle person, but with a will of steel. The diversity of his interests, his polish and manners, his air of assurance and his experience of life impressed me hugely.

I found that the young men that my mother promoted were boring in their conversations, clumsy in their attempts at seduction and could not be compared with Ted. He had become a very important part of my life.

Chapter Fourteen – Becoming Famous

I traveled up to London to have portrait photographs taken. Several agencies had commissioned these for their libraries. The Press were asking for photographs to go with various articles about me. While I was up there, I discovered Fortnum and Mason and perched on a high stool, somewhat nervously, and drank a cup of coffee surveying the scene and looking to see how everyone was dressed. I began to feel rather sophisticated and I bought a pair of high-heeled shoes with pointy toes in Bond Street which were all the rage.

Then I went to Birmingham for my first wireless broadcast and was interviewed by Roland Orton in a sports programme. He asked all the usual questions about why I had not gone to the Stockholm Olympics with Chips. I tactfully dodged these loaded questions, but went on to say how marvellous Chips had been since I had bought him back. I said that I was looking forward to next Badminton for a rematch with Colonel Weldon and Kilbarry.

My first television interview was in London. I had talked to Dorian Williams with and without Chips before the TV camera at Badminton. But actually, going into a television studio was much more daunting. I was escorted there by David Satow, who had been a 'deb's delight' in his time. He was extremely handsome and with faultless manners. We arrived at the studios and I was introduced to Paul Fox, and the front man, Peter Dimmock, who was tall, dark haired, good looking and very, very smooth. He exuded confidence. I felt a little uncomfortable being the focus of attention but my few minutes on air passed quickly and I decided that being on television was quite fun.

It was in London that Ted made a definitive move to take our relationship to the next stage. He invited me out to dinner and I went to his hotel and was shown up to his room. He had been smoking cigarettes and I rather liked the smell and the taste in his mouth. His room was luxurious with a king size bed and a large bathroom. He took me into his arms and told me not to worry, everything would be alright. He loved me and would not do anything to hurt or upset me. We had dinner in his room and we chatted about other matters such as the upcoming Hunt Ball which I was to attend with himself and his daughter. I ordered hot chocolate soufflé, which was positively delicious.

The evening progressed, and we were sitting on one of the sofas and Ted turned to me and took my hand in his. "You don't have to do this if you're not sure," he said, looking straight into my eyes. "But I want to," I had replied, "it's just that I don't know what to do." In those days sex was not the popular topic it is now, and I believed that here was someone I loved who could initiate me into the mysteries. We stood up and kissed, first softly then with increasing passion. Then he broke away and led me into the bedroom where he unzipped my dress and it fell on a heap on the floor. He pressed himself against me. Now I felt very aroused, heartbeat thudding and a longing between my legs which fluttered up into my tummy.

I stepped back, determined to do something constructive instead of just standing there and dropped my underskirt from my waist, slipped out of my shoes and stockings and sat on the bed to get rid of my knickers. He reached behind me, unhooked my bra and putting his hand round my waist, lifted me up to stand against him. He was actually shaking. He looked at me and I recognised the depth of desire in his eyes, and he must have known that I was more than ready to make love with him properly for the first time. 'Let me undress', he said and disappeared into the bathroom. All Mummy's training to fold down bedspreads in a neat pattern was forgotten. I was throwing back all the covers to the end of the bed when he came out of the bathroom and I saw my first naked man.

He caught my arm and held me close again and I felt his penis grow larger and stronger against me. He knew that I was a virgin and he had told me that there might be some blood. Some people hurt, some did not. He spoke with authority and it didn't even occur to me that he had had previous experience with virgins. As the excitement mounted, I fell backwards on to the bed and he scooped up my legs so I landed in the middle, then he was there beside me, running his hands over my breasts, cupping them – which was rather a pleasant sensation – and going down my body until his right hand was between my legs sending me into shivers of anticipation and a desperate wanting. "You're very wet," he said. and I felt his fingers go inside me and move up and down, then stroke me higher up. I shuddered, but not in horror. He moved over on top of me and I felt the hardness of his penis before he guided it into me. Not many seconds later his self-control obviously deserted him, and he cried out my name several times as he moved inside me and then withdrew suddenly and ejaculated all over my tummy. There was no large hankie at the ready! I was on fire and felt I could take to this new pastime with enthusiasm. I wanted more! 'Do it again,' I said. Ted replied that having come once he needed a short rest before he was ready for a repeat session and he got up and disappeared once again into the bathroom. I waited impatiently for his return. Back he came into the bedroom and I could see that his penis had shrunk back to sleeping size.

I asked what one did to encourage another go. He seemed to think this was very funny but suggested that I try by stroking his penis upwards. Being used to stroking horses on their forehead, or their neck to soothe and calm them, I realised that this was a different challenge. I perched myself over him and worked out that the only way I could encourage this new friend to become hard and erect was to encircle it with my fingers and lift the skin up and down in a stroking movement, gently but persuasively. I was rather thrilled when it responded, I felt as if I was giving the correct 'aids' and when it was hard enough, I straddled him, like mounting a horse, and guided it into me. I moved in the same way as he had done earlier, and the sensation was ecstatic. I could see that he had closed his eyes, his teeth were clenched and almost bared, his breath was coming in short gasps and then suddenly his eyes clicked wide open and he shouted for me to get off, jerking me upwards with his arms. I was quite put out until I realised that he had come again, and all that flying sperm would be inside me. We lay there for a while, but it was getting late. I was staying at the Ladies Club and there was curfew, so I had a last kiss, then dressed and jumped into a taxi and was back in my narrow bed still tingling with memories. It was an extraordinary night and one that I would never forget. When I got back home to Lytham, I was sure that Mummy would notice that I was different. I felt as if I had joined the grown-ups club! But no-one else seemed to notice and life went on as normal.

I was asked to stay with the Marsh's again, and this time I went hunting on Blue Jeans who gave me wonderful rides. We hunted with the local Albrighton Woodland, and also drove into the depths of the Heythrop country to follow that brilliant huntsman and Master, Ronnie Wallace. He and his team were in a class of their own, and their ability to put up a fox almost as soon as they moved off was uncanny. Hunting was exhilarating, with stinging cheeks, pounding hoofs and flying fences. I began to watch the way in which hounds worked and found this rather interesting.

At one point we were galloping full-tilt across the field and an ugly ditch with sloping guard rails loomed ahead, but on we went until the first one over shouted, 'Ware wire!' The next horse crashed through the top rails, and following him, I saw the wire leap into sight where the rail was gone. We cleared the wire, but were unable to manage the spread, and my horse had landed neatly on his nose and we slid along in swimming pose for a few yards. We came to a graceful halt, and picked ourselves up, my four-legged friend with an expression of complete amazement on his face. I climbed on again, and hurried in pursuit of the advance guard, noting as I did so that the sight of my own particular fate, had deterred any more valiant attempts to follow the chase in that direction. Luckily, I had collected little or no mud, so our disgrace was not apparent to everyone. Other days came and went, with as much excitement but no more falls, and I soon became acquainted with hunt members, whose company added much to the general enjoyment of our excursions.

The Albrighton Woodland met at Dunsley itself, and that night was the Pony Club Hunt Ball. Dawn Palethorpe was mounted on Crispin and I was on Jeans. Although we had great fun during the day, all the foxes had obviously been sent postcards to warn them of our coming, and were, no doubt, sitting safely out of reach, chortling at the antics of hounds, horses and men.

I was not brought up to hunting but found it very useful for event horses. They enjoyed jumping as a group across country. They really revelled in leaping over hedges and ditches and gates as they appeared before them. Many a sour and fed up steeplechaser has been restored to new zest for racing after a season in the hunting field. I met with nothing but friendliness whilst I was out with the hunt members. And if a horse made a mistake and took a fall, someone would catch it and bring it back to the rider.

One night during my stay I had gone to my own room at the end of the evening and was undressing to get into bed, there came a soft knock on the door. I opened it and in stepped Ted, quickly shutting the door behind him. "You must be mad," I said. I had accepted all that he had told me regarding the situation and agreement between his wife and himself. But I thought it very dangerous and asking for trouble that he was in my room. He replied, "It's perfectly alright. She is out of the way." I could hardly argue with him over that, and there was also the fact that after our last meeting in London I was just as anxious to repeat the performance as he was. He shut me up with a long kiss and started to take off my clothes. I was at a distinct disadvantage here. As soon as I saw him, the wanting flared up, despite my worry and I finished undressing myself. All the time I had my ears on end waiting for a demanding knock on the door. I decided to ignore the danger. Ted was right beside me, in a minute we would be in that single bed, and I desperately wanted him to make love to me as he had done in London. By the look of him he was on the point of exploding before he was even on top of me and I pulled off the top covers. We both shot on to the bed and very nearly fell straight off which made me laugh until he shushed me.

There was little time for foreplay. He felt between my legs which I had already opened, and I realised that he was in a real hurry. Instinctively, I extended my arms out sideways to lift my pelvis and slid straight on to his penis. He moved violently inside me, in such a hurry, and as he came, he withdrew and then he produced his hankie, like a rabbit out of a hat. He must have had an awful lot of practice to think of everything under these circumstances. This should have made me realise what type of a man he was, but in my youthful innocence I believed that we loved each other.

Ted offered to let me have Blue Jeans to school and produce for the spring trials. I discussed this with my parents. It seemed a good idea. There was another box next to Chips at Lytham Hall and it would give me the chance of a beautiful horse for the novice classes. I began work straight away on Jean's dressage. He had a very hard mouth. I had to ride him in such a way as to persuade him that I was not going to hang on to his mouth. We spent the first few weeks walking and trotting in the field, practising transitions up and down, and persevering until we were able to produce regular paces and maintain rhythm and impulsion on turns and circles. Then I asked for slower paces, and a lengthening of stride in preparation for extended work. Sometimes I would return to the stable well satisfied with his progress. On other occasions he refused to co-operate, and I suffered from tired muscles and an aching back.

Then we started work at the canter. I spent hours and hours on these transitions before he was to do them without a preliminary jerk. Then he was ready to be introduced to cavaletti. I put poles on the ground, and he trotted calmly over these for days. He had been used to working for the most part in an indoor school, so objected to the high winds, the rain and distractions our field had to offer. On fine days he would be attentive to my demands, but under adverse conditions I was nearly driven frantic by his refusals to do as I wanted.

Chips on the other hand, was beginning to get fed up with dressage so I did none with him and simply continued on with his road work to get him to the peak of fitness. All my social activities were curtailed, and I tried not to think of Ted. He telephoned often and, being an eventer himself, realised how hard I had to work to bring two horses to a state of fitness when they were both ready to win on our first outing. As Jeans became fitter, I began to doubt my ability to control him in only a straightforward snaffle bridle. I fitted him with a running martingale, which would stop him throwing his head up in the air. This worked when we were going across country. His dressage was now rather impressive, and his trot, which had been his worst pace was steady and regular. I was rather proud of this metamorphosis and could hardly wait for Ted to see him. He was also competing at Glanusk and Cottesbrooke on Wild Venture, the horse he had lent to the British Team for the Stockholm Olympics.

In preparation for Glanusk I took Jeans to a combined training event being held by our local riding club. He performed a very good dressage test, jumped beautifully and I became quite optimistic for his performance at the real thing. Then I walked him out of the stables and he was lame. I was utterly horrified. There was no visible sign to account for this, and nothing had happened. I had to break the news to Ted who was sorrier for me, than himself. No matter what I did Jeans remained lame. The vet was called, but he could not come up with anything either. I felt very responsible and extremely upset.

Plans for my twenty-first birthday were discussed and it was decided to delay the celebration until Badminton, as the majority of the people that I would like to invite would be there. We found a suitable hotel and sent out the invitations, then we realised that the date we had chosen would clash with the official Badminton Ball which was always held at the Hare and Hound Hotel at Westonbirt. My actual birthday on the 12th of March came and went quietly. Ted telephoned to wish me a happy day and I told him I would ring him on the 16th, which was his birthday. There was just four days less than 26 years between us. I had spent ages looking around in London for something suitable to give him as a gift, this was difficult as he was a man who owned everything one could possibly wish for. In the end I chose a discreet bayonet tie pin with a single pearl head. It was nothing like the expensive presents he received from other people, but he wore it for many years and always said how much he treasured it.

John's rugger career was expanding rapidly, and in addition to playing for the Harlequins, he went on to the field at Cardiff for the army, and played brilliantly, to the delight of everyone but the opposing fifteen. He had now been a member of the 'Quins for more than a season and was most anxious that the family should 'meet some of the boys' so when they had a fixture against the Waterloo Club, my parents and I were bullied into attending the game. It was a good match, with the 'Quins in winning form, and after their usual thirst-quenching at the club bar, the team was rounded up by a determined brother and introductions were made. Shades of their recent trip to Paris apparently still lingered in their minds, if the ensuing conversation was anything to go by, and their captain caused great amusement by gracefully kissing my hand in greeting and murmuring compliments in the best Gallic fashion. There were all great sports, and tremendous fun, and when at last we drove home it was with some amusing memories. Our John was at last happy to have spanned the bridge between our two so very different outdoor interests.

Chapter Fifteen – A Marriage Proposal

March gave way to April. Just before we set off for Glanusk, I went up to the British Horse Society's meeting in London. At this conference Chips was awarded leading Horse of the Year, and I was presented with the Calcutta Light Horse Challenge Cup. I won the Tony Collings Memorial Challenge Cup for the leading rider. which was an annual award. I was also awarded the Diploma of Honour. Ted and I managed to be alone in a hotel room for a few hours and then he drove me on to Glanusk to meet up with my parents who had brought Chips with them.

On the drive to Wales we talked away as usual and, suddenly he brought up the subject of marriage.

"But you're already married," I said.

"I can get a divorce," he replied, "I want to marry you."

I explained to him that the Catholic Church would not allow me to marry a divorced person and he said that was rubbish, there must be a way round. He turned off the road and stopped the car. "You are everything I want," he said, in such a way that it brought tears to my eyes. I knew that I would be a good wife for him, we got on so well in every way. We were not only lovers but also great friends, we laughed a lot and talked as equals. I could join him in all the things he enjoyed, and I certainly loved him very much. There was the age gap, but it did not worry me, and we would have such a good life.

I suddenly realised why he had taken me on a tour round the large high-walled kitchen garden whilst I was last at Dunsley. I was embarrassed to remember how I had laughed at him when he said that the Head Gardener worked really hard to produce strawberries, raspberries, peaches and asparagus for the dining table. He made a point of never going to Anglesey, or on the boat in the Mediterranean, during this period because it would cause disappointment to his employee.

He had also taken me to his private airfield, Halfpenny Green, except I had not realised that it was his property. We went up in his light aircraft and he had shown me the estate and the surrounding countryside from the air, without it even occurring to me that there must be some ulterior motive. He had invited me to take over the controls, and I was terrified at first, but he showed me what to do, demonstrating, and then just left me to fly it alone for a few minutes, and we climbed up and down a little and made a few wide turns. I rather enjoyed the feeling of being up in the high, blue sky with the ground far below, but when he said I should have lessons, it simply did not enter my head what he had in mind. I said there was no point in that as I would never be able to afford flying lessons. I remembered that he looked at me strangely but I had no idea that he wanted to marry me, and I was used to him turning to me with a quizzical eye.

Later, when he told me he wanted me to be his wife, my first reaction was that I could not imagine what my parents would say, although Daddy would be thrilled at the prospect if it meant being invited to the odd shoot. They both liked Ted, but having him as a son-in-law was a somewhat bizarre thought. My mother would respond as a good Catholic, intent only on rescuing her daughter from temptation and damnation, and she would insist on my refusing to marry a man who was not a Catholic and with a wife still under the same roof, no matter what were their arrangements. She might eventually have given way if that was all. The real sticking point would be that Ted had to obtain a divorce and that, to her, would be an impossible barrier. Daddy, too, faced a dilemma. He was not Catholic, nor was he religious, but when he married Mummy, he had given his solemn word he would not interfere with their children being brought up in the Catholic faith. That, effectively, kept him muzzled, and I very much regret that in later years I did not ask him exactly how he felt about Ted and me.

Ted stopped the car again on the drive to a restaurant that evening. Really it was so that we could continue to talk, and the conversation went around and around. What could he do to make a marriage possible? I told him that I had heard that there were some cases where an application was made to Rome for a special dispensation, undoubtedly one would have to pay! Ted pondered on this and said he would find out. We went back to the car, worry and longing all mixed up, drove on until we found a quiet spot and moved into the spacious back seat. There we made love with the passion and abandon which the situation had stirred up like a furnace, with accompanying gymnastics not made easy when dressed in smart London attire.

We arrived late at the Gliffaes hotel. My parents were settled in and had been delighted with their welcome, their large room and the setting of the house looking out over the valley with the Black Mountains as a backdrop. I had decided not to tell Mummy and Daddy about Ted before we returned to Lytham after Badminton, and probably not until he had managed to find out if there was a way around the situation. I had to focus my mind and concentrate on the event.

We had the official walk round and I saw that our old 'bogy' fence of the water splash was still part of the course. I hoped that no ugly memories would stir in the depths of Chips' mind on the next day. Chips and I were drawn number four, we did our dressage test early in the morning. We started the season well, for Chips performed a brilliant test. We went into a substantial lead. The show jumping was over a course of flimsy fences which was causing concern among the riders, and only two horses managed to go clear. Chips disgraced us by knocking down three of them and earning us thirty penalties. Our lead dropped to nine, and I was extremely annoyed both with myself and Chips. We had met all the fences on the right stride, but a trailing hoof was enough to dislodge the poles. I had a fleeting thought that perhaps it was my fault and that at the back of my mind was Ted's proposal, distracting me.

I must clear my mind. We set off round the cross-country and trying his best, Chips returned the fastest time of the day. We ended up winning from Laurien by a margin of 14.9. Had we jumped a clear round it would have been 49. It was clear to me that the new rule passed at the BHS meeting in London last November was doing what the members wanted. It was stopping me getting too far ahead.

A week later, and we were back at Cottesbrook Hall in Northamptonshire and once again I was billeted comfortably with the Head Groom and his wife, with Chips around the corner in the stable yard. Kilbarry and Weldon were declared runners, and I could hardly wait to begin. This year it was to be a two-day event with the dressage and show jumping taking part on the first day and the cross-country on the second. There were several new fences on the cross-country and of these the very first one called forth very unfavourable comment from the competitors. It was a simple straight up brushwood, frail looking, rather like a racing hurdle. It was no more than 3 feet 6 inches in height and was well and truly anchored in place by a tough horizontal telegraph pole behind it. It invited the horse to jump through it instead of over it. Realising the danger, I made a note that it needed jumping with precision and care and a take-off exactly right for its height. Just how much of an influence this fence was going to have, we had no idea.

After the dressage tests, judged by Lieutenant Commander John Oram, Chips once again led the field with only 14 penalties. I quote one of the leading newspapers: "High and Mighty was followed into the arena by Kilbarry, by no means going his best. He was rather stiff, not straight in his head, and seemed unhappy in his mouth. He did gain the useful score of 28, however. Tramella came in later, neat and fluent to score 26." In the show jumping Chips jumped a clear round as did Tramella and Pampas Cat, the latter a beautiful and talented mare who was reaching the top of her form with the very experienced rider, Kit Tatham-Warter on board. Kilbarry had two fences down, twenty penalties, giving him a total of 48, Weldon would not have been pleased with himself overnight.

Saturday was cross-country, and Chips was going fast and well. We came to a bank fence where we had to jump a post-and-rails to land towards the top of a bank, take a short stride to arrive on the downward side and then jump off half way down over a second set of post-and-rails to return again to flat ground. Chips' enthusiasm was such that his first leap took him right to the top of the bank and the next stride, even with Houdini abilities to get out of trouble, placed us impossibly close to the rails out. We almost cannoned into them. This counted as a refusal and we incurred twenty penalties. As I turned him away for a second attempt I shouted aloud my displeasure at him. With these words ringing in his ears he jumped the fence in copybook mode and finished the course in a very fast time. We had thrown away twenty penalties unnecessarily and as a result the open class was now wide open. Kilbarry, Pampas Cat and Tramella could beat me if they went clear and fast. Back at the horsebox Sheila Carden, who was acting as my groom, and I soon finished washing down Chips and then I left her to finish up whilst I set off to see what was happening on the course. Kilbarry was about to start.

I was walking along with a clear view in front of me of the first fence, with the start some way over to my right, and I heard the loudspeaker announcing that Kilbarry was being counted down. I hurried forward and stood watching as he galloped fast towards the flimsy brushwood with the telegraph pole hidden behind it. I had approached this fence very carefully and treated it like a show jump. I could hardly believe his speed. He would certainly have heard of Chips' twenty penalties and would have done his sums and realised that if he went like the wind there was a possible chance of beating us. They arrived at the fence smack on the wrong stride. Kilbarry's speed gave him no chance to 'fiddle' and his front legs cracked into the solid pole hidden behind the brush and turned him over. He described a circle in mid-air, landed on his head, as we heard later, was killed instantly.

Kilbarry had been bought by Weldon specifically as a point-to-pointer and it was possible that the horse had been confused by the speed of approach and thought he was back on a racecourse where he could brush through the top of the jump. Weldon was thrown clear but must have been devastated. My rivals were gone in a second, but this was no cause for celebration. Everyone was shocked that this legendary partnership should end in such a way. By comparison, the results hardly seemed to matter, but Pampas Cat was declared the winner, followed by Tramella, and then Chips. I was pleased when Ted moved up to fourth place on Wild Venture and Derek Allhusen was fifth on Laurien.

With Kilbarry dead there would be no duel between Weldon and myself at the Badminton Three-Day Event in two weeks' time, to which I had been looking forward so very much and for which Chips would be at his peak of fitness. My disappointment was intense, as was that of thousands of people who knew of the rivalry which existed between us. For a long time, Weldon blamed me for Kilbarry's death which was obviously blatantly untrue but showed the depth of bad feeling that existed between us. It would influence the chain of events in my life for many years.

Chapter Sixteen – Badminton, 1957

Kilbarry's death resulted in Chips being a firm favourite for the Badminton Trials, which was not a comfortable position. My parents, Sheila Carden and I set off with Chips on the long journey south. We arrived there late in the afternoon and Chips was unboxed and led into his place in the Swiss Block of stables, there to become completely at home with the exalted presence of Wild Venture next door.

During the briefing Ted sat next to me, in what I imagined to be a proprietorial way. All the competitors received their packs of map, running order and programme and listened with attention while Colonel Gordon Cox, the Trials' Director, told us that the initial entry of 57 was now down to 38 starters. He urged us to be particularly careful to keep clear of all crops and to observe the markings on the course when we came to the roads and tracks. I knew that this was directed towards me as I had taken short cuts in the past. I enjoyed pitting my wits against the course-designer, my competitive spirit could never be quelled.

Later in the afternoon all the declared runners were passed at the veterinary examination and I dashed off back to the hotel to prepare myself for a television appearance. It was the Sportsview programme, with Dorian Williams as interviewer. The few minutes passed off well enough, although my mother deflated my ego by remarking that on the screen I looked 'all squashed up'.

Perhaps she thought I needed taking down a peg or two, as on the front page of Wednesday's edition of Tatler was to be my colour photo, taken by the leading social photographer at the time, Yevonde. I was wearing my black velvet riding coat with the Union Jack stitched over my left breast, velvet cap on my head, white stock secured by a gold pin. It was very obvious that I needed my eyebrows to be tidied up but at that stage I wasn't cognisant of such elaborate grooming. It gave me a funny feeling to know that it was going to be displayed in all the railway station kiosks and shops throughout the country.

I was drawn last to go, number 55, which meant I had the morning of the Thursday dressage day free to do just the leg stretch Chips needed, no more than a little viewing of the dressage arena in front of the house and a ride round the park, keeping well away from any of the fences.

I went on a private tour of parts of the speed and endurance and then was back in time to saddle up for our dressage test. The Queen, Prince Philip and members of the Royal family sat in their tent at the side of the arena, and before we entered the ring, the steward reminded me of their presence and the bow it demanded. Just before we were due to start, waiting for the judges' signal, I asked Chips for an extended trot and was most dismayed when he misunderstood and broke into a canter instead. We came to a halt in front of the Royal tent, and bowed gracefully. Then the judges' bell rang out, and we were passing through the arena gate while a steward held its silken cord to one side, his doffed hat in hand.

Our test had begun. It was a new dressage test, this time with 18 individual sets of movements, each marked from zero to the maximum six. We moved off at a trot from centre X after saluting the three judges. Then twice went across diagonals from quarter marker to quarter marker in an extravagant and balanced extended trot, showing beautifully smooth transitions. The extremely difficult five metre half circles had been replaced by two whole circles of a far easier seven metres departing from X on the line from A. We did half-passes at collected trot, and two turns on the haunches from a four-square halt, hind legs marching in a tiny circle and the forelegs crossing over each other on the way round. We had a rein back and a canter from walk showing the difference between three canter outlines with ordinary pace, collected and extended. There was also a serpentine two yards either side of the centre line without losing the leading leg or becoming unbalanced. Chips went through the various movements with all his usual *élan* and precision, and as we made our final salute to the judges, I knew his test had been a good one. We left the arena in a storm of applause, which Chips apparently accepted calmly as his due, for he took not the slightest notice, and cantered out of the ring quite unperturbed. The laden clouds, threatening overhead throughout the afternoon, had released some sleet during our test, but luckily this had been only slight, and familiar with the weather's vagaries as he was, Chips had carried on notwithstanding.

Our marks were soon announced. We went into the lead with 24.33 penalties, second was Tramella with Diana Mason on 28.33 and Pampas Cat with Kit Tatham-Warter on 32. Ted had improved as a result of his avowed determination to watch how I worked. What I had suggested to him in his manner of riding for eventing had certainly helped and we were both thrilled with his mark of 44.67 which put him fifth, Derek Allhusen sixth on 47.33. The change in the rules meant that there was only 60 points between the first and the last competitors. The influence of the dressage test was reduced by 50 per cent. I felt this was a mistake as many of the riders only did their dressage because it was required, without really understanding the value of training for the dressage, which not only helped a horse to excel on the first day but was also of huge benefit in the jumping phases.

At the start of the second day we stood four marks ahead of our nearest rival, with the added advantage that, by the time I started on the cross-country phase of the speed and endurance, I should know how my fellow-competitors had fared. I was waiting to go in the mid-afternoon and the atmosphere was tense. The wind was so strong that I could not make out what was being said on the loudspeakers. The atmosphere around the stables was charged, full of anticipation and excitement and the crowds milled around the tents downing drinks and eating lunch deciding from which vantage points they wanted to watch on the cross-country.

Chips was given a token half scoop of lightly crushed best oats at mid-morning and his water bucket was taken away at one o'clock in the afternoon. Sheila Carden and I would be screwing in the sharp studs rather than the round or square ones.

Chips and I started off along phase A just after three o'clock. It was bitterly cold, but as far as we were concerned this was all to the good. The fierceness of the wind made it difficult to judge speed on the steeplechase course, and we did not go quite fast enough to gain maximum bonus points. However, by the time we arrived in the enclosure with five minutes in hand, Chips showed no signs of fatigue and when I jumped up again to come under starter's orders, he was full of energy and keener than ever to be off.

We shot away at a great gallop, over the first four fences, the fifth with its awkward approach, and then the Vicarage Ditch, modified from the last year's version but still an enormous obstacle. We sailed this jump very flamboyantly and I felt so proud of Chips. Continuing on at full speed - the giant Irish Bank, the water jump, and the troublesome Luckington Road Crossing behind us. We thundered on round the course, over the Coffin, never putting a foot wrong; the Quarry, with its fearsome drop, felt as nothing with Chips in his present mood, and soon the Lake Fence came in sight, and we were over with hardly a foot wet, so quickly did he turn and race towards the finish. I jumped off in the unsaddling enclosure and took the saddle with me for 'weighing-in'.

As I stood on the scales the steward saw a Land Rover pull to a stop – the one in which the Royal party were following competitors' fortunes. I was terrified lest I should be summoned in my present state, for I was dying to blow my nose. All was well, however, for to my relief only a message was brought over with the kind query as to whether Chips had finished free from penalty. Princess Margaret took a cine film of Chips as he was led away from the enclosure. I followed on to the stables by car as soon as the results came through and it was known we had received full bonus points for the course.

My brother, John, had joined us at Badminton, on leave from his army duties, and many of our northern friends had already arrived and were also staying at the hotel ready to enjoy my party on the night of the speed and endurance. After being sure that Chips was sound and in good spirits, my parents, John and I left Chips and Patch in the safe hands of Sheila Carden and made a dash to the hotel where my first job was to wash and set and dry my hair, then have a bath and present myself downstairs as the party girl before the guests arrived.

In those days, party dress was formal. Our friends would be wearing black tie or tails or long evening dresses and gloves, and it took some time to get ready. John and a friend from his regiment had the job of making sure that every guest as they entered the ballroom was given a name badge to be pinned on them. The guests were eventers, northerners, some horsey and some not. We wanted to ensure they would mix and talk to each other. Mummy had also said that it would aid Daddy's unreliable memory for names, all he had to do was read the label. His eyesight was fine. When everyone had arrived, we all trooped into the dining room for dinner and on each side-plate sat a stick of Blackpool Rock and a hot bread roll.

The stick of rock caused great amusement when it was discovered that the inscription through the middle of the stick read "Rock and Roll at Sheila's Twenty-First". I am sure the southerners thought this very peculiar at first sight until they realised the implication of the rock and the roll on each plate, and towards the end of the party one of them was heard bleating plaintively that her stick of rock had disappeared from the window sill on which she had left it. We had to find her another.

I had been at one particular party in the Midlands with Ted and his daughter Judy, and Duncan whom she was to marry, and had been very impressed with the band there. When it came to us finding a band for the party, I had suggested them to my parents who quickly booked them to play at my twenty-first. They played waltzes and quicksteps and tangos equally as well as the current penchant of the young for rock and roll.

When we met in London, sometimes Ted would take me to the 'in' night attractions, and I had discovered that he had a real sense of rhythm. He was a very good dancer, and this was definitely a turn on. But when I danced with him that night, he became a different person, totally correct, infinitely charming, but careful to hold me at a distance. I teased him about this attitude and asked him what was wrong, and his reply was that we had to do this in public until he knew whether or not we could be married. I understood but was momentarily sad. It also occurred to me that eventers and organisers would have to be pretty blind not to notice that there was something between us when we were at competitions. We both believed it was only a matter of time and money before word came that the Church would allow us to marry. We even discussed the topic of children, but he said that he already had two, and wanted to have me all to himself!

At midnight I was presented with an enormous key, by virtue of Daddy's carpentry skills, and then the specially made cake was cut and handed round to all our guests. My parents had used Daddy's confectionery contacts to have made a king of a cake, a real work of art. The top showed a cross-country course, complete with a yellow castle, pale blue streams and undulating terrain, and there were twenty-one fences, each representing a year of my life, and a little model of Chips and me leaping safely over the last one. It was brilliant and showed how much thought and love had gone into their preparations for my party. It brought tears to my eyes.

The party was due to finish at half past two in the morning, but at three o'clock we were still trying to shoo away the lingering few. I could hardly keep upright. The party had been an undoubted success, thanks to my parents planning and their generosity, and next morning when I was crawling round Badminton with eyes half shut, it was lovely to hear the guests discussing the evening as a really good time and well worth the journey. My parents received some lovely thank you letters.

By twelve o'clock I was dressed ready for the final show jumping phase. I went up to the arena and walked the course which was very twisty but at least the fences looked solid instead of flimsy. Anything could happen. Spectators already in their seats called out 'Good luck'. I smiled back in thanks and resolved we must not let anyone down. The parade of horses and riders still in the competition was due to start at two o'clock and would proceed in the starting order of the first day. I was the last to go. Chips and I brought up the rear as we made our way around the ring, passed the Royal Box, giving a salute, and exiting back into the collecting ring. There was a plan of the show jumping course pinned up on a board beside the weighing tent and I spent a good few minutes studying it and making sure I knew the way round. Victory lay within our grasp and I must not do anything silly, like taking the wrong course. I knew how my nearest competitors had done before I went into the ring, but a long wait, with the crowd either bursting into applause for a clear round or groaning as a fence fell, was a challenge and I had to keep calm and resolved.

Ted with Wild Venture knocked down two fences, but the Irish Penny Moreton jumped a clear round and when at last it was time for Chips to go into the ring, I knew that we had two fences in hand. Each fence down meant a penalty of 10 marks. In the collecting ring Sheila had set up the practice fence for me and I deliberately brought Chips towards it on the wrong stride. He hit it and I growled at him and took him in on the correct stride and when he cleared it, I made a great fuss of him.

We went into the ring did a preliminary circle at canter bowed to the Queen and the Royal party. Nearly all the competitors had hit the fifth fence, an awkwardly sited in-and-out. As we sailed over the fourth jump I tried to impress on Chips how he must concentrate on the next obstacle. His ears flicked back as I took a stronger hold on his mouth and I closed my legs to emphasise that he must be careful. We met it on a perfect stride and sailed over the first part, I gave him a tiny check to shorten the first of the two strides he would take between the in and out fences and he was over the second part with ease. We sailed over numbers six and seven with a clean pair of heels and coming in to the eighth, an upright, I nearly had a heart attack because we were between strides. Either he must take off early or get very close and knock it straight down. I told him to take off and he completely ignored me. From right underneath, he performed the most extraordinary acrobatic jump I have ever experienced in the saddle. He went up and down like a lift, clearing the gate completely and landing with all four feet together, safe on the other side. It was Houdini at his best. There were still four fences to jump, but these we negotiated without further excitement and a clear round was announced. The laurels of last year's elusive Badminton had become ours for 1957, and back into the ring we went as soon as I had been weighed in. Chips stood at the head of the prize-winners. I had to dismount to go forward to receive our trophies and rosettes from the Queen. She was clearly interested and completely natural and said to me that she still could not believe that Chips could have cleared that gate from where he had taken off and thought he must be a very clever horse. I replied that he was a horse in a million.

At last I was back on Chips and cantering round the ring in front of the other prize-winners, cheeks flushed with a mixture of pride and relief. I was even nasty enough to think again of those men at Windsor making such a mess of riding Chips, and hoped they were feeling embarrassed. We had won by a margin of 25.79 marks, not a bad lead when one takes into account the new rule designed to reduce the influence of the dressage. Penny Moreton moved up into second place by courtesy of her clear round, and Ted dropped to third on Wild Venture as a forfeit for knocking down two fences. Gillian Morrison on Benjamin Bunny finished fourth with one fence down. Unusually, there were only four clear rounds on the last day of the show jumping, Penny and I, and the two riders in fifteenth and twenty-first places, Virginia Freeman-Jackson and Captain Sworder.

The Times correspondent wrote: "Looking the picture of fitness, High and Mighty took the parallel bars cleverly, got under the gate but was saved by his pony cleverness and somehow twisted over it and finished brilliantly to win a victory which has been his due since last season. As to his rider, it can only be said that, if it is possible, she has improved in this year and we are grateful to her for setting such an admirable standard". Also, one of the leading newspapers: "Badminton without Kilbarry could not be quite the same, and we were robbed of what might have been a Homeric contest. However, Miss Sheila Willcox and High and Mighty were worthy winners all the way, perhaps the most efficiently stylish exhibition ever of the series. It was a fitting celebration for her twenty-first birthday." In *Country Life*: "As I watched the superlative display of training given with what appeared to be effortless enjoyment by Sheila Willcox and the beautiful and co-operative High and Mighty in the dressage test on the first day, it occurred to me that the alteration in the value of the dressage marking might also penalise the all-round perfect performer in favour of the horse and rider who were good in many ways but not all." And lastly by Henry Wynmalen, a man of impeccable credentials for his ability as a judge in world dressage competition: "Finally, the last competitor to appear before the judges, Sheila Willcox riding High and Mighty, who produced a superb performance to assume the lead which she was to retain unchallenged to the end. Her presentation was almost faultless, ridden with impeccable assurance, and would have been difficult to beat in any company." I valued these comments, and even wondered how Chips and I had managed to be where we were when we had been through so many trials and traumas. I was only the second woman to win the Badminton Three-Day Event, the first being Margaret Hough who had taken us to our first one-day event at Hovingham just eighteen months ago. We also equalled the record of Frank Weldon who had been the only person to have won both the Badminton and the Harewood Trials.

The television people asked us to go straight to their camera vans, and with Mummy and a crowd of reporters and well wishers in hot pursuit, Chips and I made our way to be interviewed. We had just reached our destination, with Dorian Williams waiting for us when the Royal Land Rover drove past and the Queen and her family opened windows and waved. Dorian unravelled his yards of wire and with microphone in hand he stood beside me on Chips talking about our win with the eye of the camera focused on the three of us. Chips became so excited with the pressing crowd that he started to dance about, and Dorian had to keep hopping out of range of his hoofs. I found it hard to keep a straight face. The interview ended, and Chips was surrounded by his fans. He rather fancied all this attention. Then I said I must take him back to his stable and bidding everyone farewell we made our way back. Soon we would be all packed up and ready to leave Badminton for a second time to return to Lytham, but this year it would be under our own colours with Chips safe in the back, surrounded by an aura of glory.

Badminton, 1957. Sitting next to Ted Marsh for the briefing of competitors. Kit Tatham-Warter is on the other side of Ted. Also, in the photo are Jeremy Beale, Isobel Touche, Shirley Clifford, Ian Dudgeon, Penny Moreton, Gillian Morrison and Susan Fitzroy.

The Lake Fence behind us, we splash towards dry land and the run i

Speed and endurance day at Badminton, 1957. Halfway over the Timber Wagon, and already looking eagerly for the next fence.

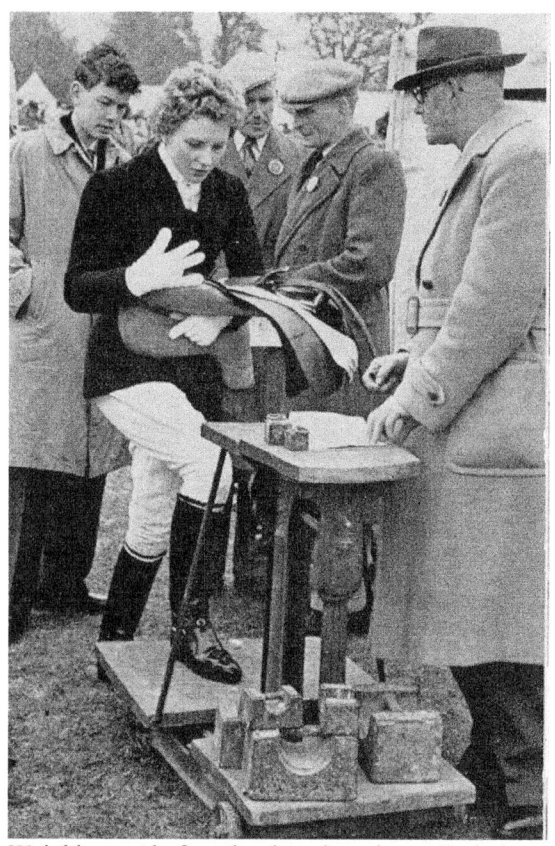

Weighing out before the show jumping at Badminton. The weight did not quite warrant my horrified expression.

The veterinary inspection at Badminton before the final show jumping phase. While the Queen looks on, Chips is walked up by Sheila Carden, his groom for the week.

The walk-round at Harewood, 1957. I decide where Chips and I will jump and try it out for myself.

Chapter Seventeen – Riding for England

Everyone at home was delighted with our success, and it was decided by the local Council that I should be invited to the Mayor's Parlour and received an inscribed crop to commemorate the occasion and a photograph was taken for the local newspaper. What a shame that the one who really merited such attention could not taste all these fruits of victory; but then, after all, perhaps Chips would rather have been where he was enjoying the luscious spring grass, and the unaccustomed freedom to wander at will, with a herd of cows and their master the bull for company, and nothing to do day after day but eat, sleep and eat again. Every day I rode my bicycle up to take him a bucket of oats. He was dreamy and contented and I would sit beside him and stroking his neck, tell him that time was passing, and his holiday would not go on forever.

The leading literary agents in London had asked me to write my autobiography and Mummy insisted that I work on it every morning. I was virtually locked in the dining room from half past eight until lunchtime, writing in longhand and eventually using my fading secretarial skills to send a typed copy to George Greenfield of John Farquarson Ltd, later amalgamated with Curtis Brown. This book was first published in 1958. It was well received and sold all over Europe and I had money to spend for the first time.

When I visited London, George would take me out to lunch at Quaglinos. He wanted me to go to the States with him on a book tour but Mummy vetoed this in no uncertain terms. George said that I wrote well and wanted me to follow in Pat Smythe's footsteps and produce children's books like her pony books about herself and three invented young people, 'the Three Jays'. But I didn't have that sort of imagination and I was too busy riding.

I did write the Foreword for one edition of 'The Horsemasters' by Don Stanford. I loved this novel as it not only had a good story, but was bursting with accurate information about riding and training horses. Later when I could not ride after my accident, I worked on a second autobiography *Winning is Everything*, which picked up from the end of *Three Days Running*. It has now been published by Epona Publishing and can be purchased through Amazon.

I also wrote *The Event Horse* that covers every aspect of purchasing and training an eventing horse based on my own experience. An e-book version of it has been re-published by Epona Publishing and can be purchased through Amazon. In the 1970s, *The Event Horse* was filmed and shown on television three times.

Over the years I have written the complete story behind *Three Days Running* and included a more truthful account of my personal life and the corruption and politics in the sport of eventing run by a patriarchy of arrogant men. This publication of *Three Days Running* has been significantly revised and added to and is no longer the sort of book to be found in a school library!

Back in July 1957, I brought Chips in to work again before the flies began to torment him. He had rested for longer than I had planned. Meanwhile, there had come a letter from the British Horse Society inviting Chips and me to train for the European Trials which would take place at the beginning of October. I accepted at once, for I was thrilled at the prospect of going to Windsor again for a month or so, but this development caused me to make changes in the plans I had already thought out for the season. Ted had also been invited with Wild Venture and he and I were tickled pink at the prospect of having six weeks together at the hotel on Windsor High Street. Previously, I had intended to give Chips only a month's rest after Badminton, and then bring him in so that he would be fit enough to take to the Brickett Wood tests just before the opening of the International Horse Show in July. Now I decided to forgo these events, and leave Chips out for a little longer as then he would come to his peak fitness much later, something which I considered very necessary in view of the changed schedule.

I worked out a training programme with this in mind, so eventually Chips was brought in at the beginning of July, and we started on the task of reducing him to his former weight and a more sylph-like figure. For the first fortnight we took only gentle exercise until his legs became accustomed to working on the hard ground again, and then each morning there was dressage practice to be done and week by week the length and pace of his road work was increased.

By August, Chips had begun to look more like his old self. Most of his surplus flesh was gone, the gentle exercise had hardened his legs, and he was in an altogether better condition. I decided that it would be a good thing for us to take part in a few jumping competitions before the assembly date at Windsor. We went to several local shows, either as a jumper, or as a Working Hunter – a class judged half on the horse himself and half on his performance over fences. Chips excelled in these, and on each occasion won the red rosette. Our jumping prowess, however, was not as spectacular, but my aim of practice was fulfilled, and as the date for our Windsor departure drew near, I felt both Chips and I were sufficiently prepared to withstand the rigours of collective training.

Seven horses and riders were being considered by the BHS Selection Committee for inclusion in the Copenhagen team, but even before we assembled, one of them dropped out. Penelope's horse, Bandoola strained a tendon and had to be rested just at the crucial moment. But then only three days before we should have traveled south, Colonel Weldon telephoned to say that the start of training was postponed. As acting non-riding Captain, he would be responsible for the training schedule during the six-week period. Most unfortunately, he had been trodden upon by a young horse and as a result his right leg was encased in plaster. For at least a week, riding – and even walking – was out of the question, he would be quite unable to supervise us at Windsor in that condition – and that was that. My disappointment was acute, for I had been eagerly awaiting our time in the south. However, there was nothing to be gained by doing other than wait patiently for the passing of the next ten days, and meanwhile I continued with the task of producing Chips in a fit state to perform at the Melton Mowbray Trials.

At last it was time to lead him up the horsebox ramp and set off for Leicestershire. The official 'walk-round' took place in the afternoon, and I joined my fellow competitors to view the course on foot. It was much the same as that of the previous year, but with the added difficulty that the largest grass field had been put under plough. This meant that the horses would have to work twice as hard to get over the furrows, and I was a little worried lest Chips should object and try to register his disapproval.

The weather was good for this opening autumn trials competition. Chips and I followed Margaret Hough's Bambi in the open dressage arena. Again, he went really well – and at the end of the first phase we were in the lead. Show jumping came next – a dreadful course, full of twists and turns, and obviously extremely difficult. As I cantered Chips about outside the ring, I watched the early numbers go around the course, and was horrified to see how few managed to clear all the fences. Then Laurien did a clear round but even she had time penalties, though she seemed to fly. I decided Chips would really have to exert himself if we were to emerge unpenalised, and when we eventually took our turn, we were absolutely determined that he should manage it.

After the first fence I realised thankfully that he was going to jump well then, without losing a second, I was concentrating on turning him for the next. His natural hardiness came to the fore; we lost no time in between fences, and when we were over the last one, we cantered out with no penalties. Only the cross-country remained, and I hoped Chips would still be in a good mood when he had to start. The previous year he had been most unwilling to go across country and I had had to work really hard to force him towards the first fence. This time, however, he seemed inclined to take more interest in the proceedings and galloped over the first post-and-rails in great heart. On we went, right-handed down the hill and over a rail set high in a wide ditch – a very nasty jump. Soon we were in the plough, then out and over more fences in the open country, before jumping back into the ploughed field. This time its heaviness began to take its toll, and Chips was puffing as we made our way up the incline towards a big trakehner fence. To my relief he jumped it well despite his weariness, and, landing on grass again we both breathed freely as the ground sloped away in front of us. The last few fences presented no difficulty and in a minute our autumn debut was over. It only remained for Chips to be sponged, rubbed down and made comfortable for the night, while I recovered more quickly to watch how other competitors fared over the course. Gillian Morrison, Jeremy Beale and Derek Allhusen were also taking part in the open section with Chips and me. The four of us were to join Kit Tatham-Warter and Ted at Windsor the following day, so as future collaborators we rejoiced when the results showed us in the leading places. Chips had won for the second year running.

I traveled to Windsor in the wake of the horsebox to find Chips already ensconced in the Royal Mews with the other five horses. His box was the same as before Stockholm, and I shuddered at the prospect of a repeat performance of that fiasco. Chips, however, seemed perfectly happy. Certainly, he was none the worse for his

Melton activities, and the following morning seemed quite excited at the prospect of exercise in Windsor Great Park. It is a marvellous training-centre there: miles and miles of suitable roads and tracks for fittening work, space to gallop, and flat paddocks for dressage and jumping. We were more than indebted to the Queen for her generosity in allowing us to make use of such amenities.

Throughout the first week horses and riders were left more or less to their own devices. Fate seemed to be against us at the offset for Gillian's two horses Benjamin Bunny and Just William were unsound from the Melton Trials. She spent all day every day sitting on a bench spraying gallons of water over offending legs in an effort to cure the trouble.

Colonel Weldon would accompany us on his new horse when we went to gallop, and would take the lead, to set the pace. All the horses but Chips were Thoroughbreds and much faster on the flat than we were, so we always finished well in the rear.

The sound horses were given dressage instruction each day by Robert Hall and then we went out, singly or otherwise, for ordinary exercise. Chips and I soon found ourselves going out alone, for my method of getting him fit differed greatly from those of the other four. At home we have to stay on hard roads most of the time as there were no wide-open spaces on which to enjoy an occasional canter. Thus, Chips had become accustomed to trotting along for mile upon mile. Before long at Windsor our progress would be greeted with cries of "Where's the milk-float?" – remarks to which Chips luckily took no exception.

I was fascinated by the little grey squirrels which run all over the park, and once I caught a glimpse of a big red fox who seemed almost as stunned as I was by our encounter. The Long Walk, the Copper Horse, Royal Lodge, Smith's Lawn and Virginia Water all became familiar sights.

It was fun having other women there, Gillian and I got on very well. Kit was older than us but would talk to us when it suited her. She was from an old army family and her brother was famous for going into battle with his umbrella. She, herself had served in the Second World War as an ambulance driver and received the *Croix de Guerre*. Jeremy was young and very easy to get along with and put up with us pulling his leg. Then there was Ted, but he had to keep rushing away to Calne and keep Marsh and Baxters from not collapsing without him. He did however sneak back every night to find time for our sexual exploits, which were somewhat curtailed by my small single room and narrow bed and the fact that one of the team members might decide they wanted to ask me something.

By this time only four of the original seven horses were fit to go north. Bunny was still lame, and Fulmer Folly had joined him in the sick bay. That left Chips, Laurien, Venture and Pampas Cat still on four legs, and Just William recovered sufficiently to accompany them to Harewood. It had been decided that the four horses should take part in the trials in a non-competitive capacity – a real disappointment to us all, and especially to me, for I had been looking forward tremendously to retaining the Harewood crown.

Chips and I were there but had no chance of repeating our win. It seemed strange to watch the trials progress from the side lines, and I must admit I didn't enjoy the experience. However, we four had to do the dressage and cross-country phases to give the Selectors some idea of our form, so after the proper competitors had finished, we performed the Copenhagen dressage test. Laurien and Pampas Cat went before Chips, and Venture came in last.

Chips was in a brilliant mood and gave me such a good ride that I even had time to watch the illuminated board which showed our various marks. This was connected to the judges' tent, and as each mark for a movement was given by the judge, his secretary would press a corresponding bell and the number would flash on the board outside for all to see. Almost at the end of the test we came to a halt to do the difficult 'see-saw' movement – six paces backwards, four forwards, six back and halt. Chips did this beautifully but must have been so busy congratulating himself that he had no time to take notice of the fact that I was frantically telling him to move off at a canter. My leg nearly fell off with the effort of giving him exaggerated aids, and then at last he realised I wanted something, and he stumbled feebly forward eventually to break into a canter. Luckily it was his only lapse, and so hardly affected our total marks, but it was a warning to me of the dreadful things which can happen in a test. We must definitely not repeat it in Copenhagen, I vowed, even if it meant practising the movement until we did it in our sleep.

The speed and endurance course had been extremely well designed and the cross-country phase, in particular, was absolutely first-class. It included some very awkward obstacles, and the fence into the lake was obviously to prove something of a problem. There were two alternatives to it. The easier was a low post-and-rails approached down a bank, with a very suspicious-looking marshy strip of ground as take-off on the edge of the lake. The other was much higher, with a similar take-off, but facing water on the landing side which looked feet deep. If only one had some means of communicating to the horse that it was only inches to solid bottom! I puzzled over these alternatives for a long while, and eventually decided to play safe and make for the smaller obstacle. It had been sited in such a way that taking this would result in a loss of time, but I considered it a far better proposition than to run the risk of a refusal at the bigger fence.

We four were again to follow the rest of the competitors, so as soon as the steeplechase course was clear we went singly over a few fences to get our horses jumping well and strongly. Then we went to the cross-country collecting ring, and so that Chips would know what was to come, Pat Robson (the girl acting as Chips' groom) washed him down just as if he had been competing properly. It seemed to have the desired effect for Chips became most excited, and by the time we were ready he was longing to be off. The first few fences were much the same as the last year's, but there was a tricky new one sited at the end of an old silage pit which had to be approached either down a steep drop from the side or from the far end over a post-and-rails. I chose the latter way, and we were in and out without a second wasted, then the ha-ha into the wood faced us, the sheer walled drop of five feet into the lane, and over another stone wall before emerging at the Quarries.

It was the most wonderful feeling all the way round the course, for Chips never put a foot wrong and seemed to jump effortlessly. In no time we were galloping towards the lake, and as we turned to take the smaller fence, I sat down harder in the saddle ready to give Chips an extra push. Down the bank we went and over the rail into the water before I even realised it. Then we were proceeding in a series of leaps and bounds towards the far bank, and by the time we had jumped the fallen tree-trunk to make for the last fence, I was thoroughly soaked and had swallowed pints of the water. We sailed over the last obstacle and I felt Chips tire beneath me as we made our way uphill to the finishing post. Then it was all over, and I dismounted to pat Chips and watch him washed down. So, for us the Trials were finished, for a decision had already been made that we should not show jump on the last day. Instead, we watched Gillian, on her second horse Just William lose her overnight lead to Ian Dudgeon on his father's Charleville, and so saw the conclusion of a Harewood at which we had been neither competitors nor onlookers.

Back at Windsor again, we all settled down to a routine of dressage work and long exercise, interspersed with show jumping instruction from Jack Talbot-Ponsonby, and twice-weekly gallops under the watchful eye of Colonel Weldon. Bunny, Willie and Fulmer Folly still stood for long sessions under the hosepipe, and then misfortune turned in another direction, and first Laurien, then Chips, Cat and Venture went down with a flu germ. Chips caught its most virulent form and produced symptoms of jaundice to our greatest alarm. He was dosed with powders wrapped in strawberry jam, for some days, and obviously felt very sorry for himself. Then he began to recover, and by the end of the week was his old self again. We began to resume hard work.

A mere fortnight separated us from departure for Copenhagen, and in that time horses and riders became more and more fit. Chips' illness had delayed my training schedule by only a few days, for I had intended to give him half a week's gentle exercise on our return from Harewood. I consoled myself that at least he'd caught the germ at the best possible time.

Dressage work continued daily under Robert Hall's instruction and Jack Talbot-Ponsonby's two visits were of immense value. He is a brilliant instructor and seems able to pick out faults in horse and rider after a minute's scrutiny, and suggest the remedy in simple, sound terms. His second visit to Windsor was on a dreadful day. Willie, Cat, Laurien, Venture and Chips had to perform in torrential rain. Chips and I were last to go, but despite the conditions, he jumped freely and well. I had been doing some cavaletti work each morning before breakfast, and felt sure that this had helped enormously to strengthen and supple him. Unlike the Turin training period, we had no lungeing, nor supervised cavaletti work, but as the cavalettis were there it seemed stupid not to take advantage of their presence. When dressage work was over, Chips and I went into the indoor school and played there together over the cavalettis, doing a tremendous amount of good and thoroughly enjoying ourselves in the process.

There was one more public appearance before we left for Copenhagen – at the Camberley Show. Laurien and Chips competed in the Medium Dressage Test while Cat and Willie did the Elementary, and we all jumped in the show-ring. The day before this, Venture had gone lame. We had all finished our gallop together and returned to the stables. Venture was definitely going 'short', so all hopes of his competing at Camberley the next day had to be abandoned. Luckily, however, he had only knocked himself and in a matter of days he was perfectly sound again.

I had never done the Medium Test before Camberley, but our debut into the dressage world was marked by my first lapse of memory. Halfway through the test I cantered blithely on round the arena, when I should have circled – and the bell rang to indicate an error of course. Luckily, I didn't have to stop for the judges to tell me where the *faux pas* had occurred, and Chips went on quite unperturbed. He had done another brilliant test despite my lapse and was later rewarded when the first rosette was clipped on to his bridle. Laurien, Willie and Chips jumped clear rounds in the show-ring, so our day was complete but as we were there only for practice we decided not to jump off against the other unpenalised horses, and instead returned to Windsor and the Mews for a final wind-up in the training programme.

Dressage day at Harewood. Chips and I go through the Olympic trials test in preparation for Copenhagen a month later.

The Olympic trials test at Harewood in preparation for Copenhagen.

Cross-country at Harewood. Water flies in all directions as we leap the 'hazard' fence to save precious seconds.

Chips leads the string down the Long Walk at Windsor.

Selected to ride for Britain again. Chips and I pictured at Windsor.

Chapter Eighteen – Jumping for Gold

The team for Copenhagen was announced at last, and Chips was one of the four. Venture, Cat, and Laurien were the others, with Willie going as an individual. On the Monday preceding the Trials we were all up at the crack of dawn and traveled to Blackbushe Airport before breakfast. Take-off was to be at nine-thirty, but the hour came and went and still we were not airborne. Then we learnt that our overall weight was over half a ton in excess of the plane's capacity, and until we managed to lose those extra pounds, we should have to stay grounded. First, we thought of sending several of the twelve bodies by ordinary passenger flights, but that idea was discarded when we realised the difference would be infinitesimal. In the end we had to resign ourselves to leaving behind the three huge hampers containing the horses' gear, all their fodder – and even, when, the weight still had to be reduced, some of our own luggage. The prospect of arriving in Copenhagen with nothing for the horses and what they stood up in, plus their grooming bags, was somewhat alarming, but we hoped the freight plane would deliver the rest of the gear by the following morning. With all this arranged we trooped out thankfully to the waiting plane. Venture was loaded first, Chips followed and was manoeuvred into the stall next to him, then Cat, Willie and Laurien walked up the ramp, and the nose of the plane was closed. The rest of us settled in the passenger compartment, and at last we were off.

The flight lasted six hours, and by the end of the first two I was beginning to wish I'd never set foot in an aeroplane, Ted who was a holder of a pilot's licence, assured me we were not experiencing bumps it was 'merely the effect of the wind' – but I was at a stage when I could not have cared less about any whys and wherefores. Our arrival at Amsterdam saved me just in the nick of time. The plane was refuelled both there and at Hamburg, then, as the light began to fade, we touched down at Kastrup – and we had arrived in Copenhagen.

The Trials organisers met us at the airport and I had my first taste of Danish charm and hospitality. In no time we were through Customs and following the horses on their way to Charlottenlund, a trotting stadium where all the Trials' horses were being stabled. Chips was tired after the long journey, and obviously delighted at being left to rest. At last, the stable doors were shut, and we all drove off to the hotel to prepare ourselves for the rigours of the competition ahead.

The Polish Team arrived the next day with their horses then the French, the Germans, the Swedes, and the Danes themselves. An Irish Team had been entered, but in the end did not come owing to lameness and difficulty with quarantine restrictions on return to Ireland. However, the cosmopolitan flavour was truly present, and I, for one, was in my element. We exercised the horses on the grass centre of the trotting stadium, and Chips' eyes nearly popped out of his head in amazement at the sight of the racing ponies flying round the track with their sulkies. The Charlottenlund stables house a large number of these ponies, and each morning one can see the trainers introducing youngsters to their metier or putting the older hands through their paces. I was longing to have a go with one of them, but no opportunity presented itself.

The fact that half our grooms were girls aroused open-mouthed astonishment in the stable yard. That they should be capable of looking after a horse appeared to be completely beyond the imagination of the other grooms, and the sight of our three mucking out in the mornings almost brought Charlottenlund to a standstill. I simply cannot imagine what would have been thought had they known how many English girls combine the activities of owner, rider and groom.

The veterinary examination was at eight o'clock on the Wednesday morning, and all 27 starters were declared fit to take part. Then it was time for us to see the speed and endurance course, and eventually we were all settled in cars and driven along the two phases of roads and tracks. Both A and C were along hard roads, with little opportunity of leaving them for the relief of grass verges and tracks. Chips' milk-float trot was going to come in useful. We had to climb out of the cars halfway round phase C, for there we reached the confines of the Deer Park, where motors were not allowed. We transferred to horse-drawn carriages, and this was great fun for we bowled along in fine style, much more able to appreciate the beauties of the countryside.

The steeplechase course was left as our last viewing phase, for during the morning there would be racehorses on the track, so as soon as we came to the end phase C, we set off on foot to inspect the horrors of the cross-country course. The first fence was alright – a mere post-and-rails, and from a distance the second looked almost as innocuous. However, that turned out to be wishful thinking, for on reaching it we found that the ground on landing dropped away into a steep slide, and that almost at the bottom of it was another stiff post-and-rails, making our task even more difficult. The next one to cause me some disquiet was number seven, a 'pedestrian crossing' fence – parallel bars, broken alternately by narrow spaces which made the problem of approach very awkward. Then a combination fence, set at right angles, numbers ten, eleven and twelve, and this was obviously going to prove troublesome. One had to turn sharply to the first element off the existing track, only a few yards away, or swing farther out under a belt of trees before approaching the obstacle.

The fence itself consisted of a post-and-rails with a ditch on the landing side, and then one had to turn first right, over some sheep racks, and then sharp left over more tracks, a few paces away, before reaching open country again. Later in the course there was another nasty combination fence over banks, and a big open ditch and rails following it, I began to worry when I realised the type of course it was – definitely a galloping one, for there were groups of fences and then long stretches before the next lot. I felt that on such a course Chips would be at a distinct disadvantage against the bigger, faster animals.

Farther on, there was a very difficult quarry type combination of three fences, sited in a ravine. It started with rails set on the edge of the steep, slippery, almost sheer slide, then there was a big trakehner over a wide ditch, and at the top of a correspondingly steep slope were more rails absolutely on the shelf of the ravine. These three fences, and the next, a big garden boundary fence with a five-foot drop on to a hard track, were enough to give me no sleep for the next two nights; and the last fences, a solid triple bar into deep water, and a post-and-rails out of the same depth, did nothing to cheer me up.

Other members of the Team did not seem unduly distressed by the course, and as usual I refused to commit myself to an opinion of it as a whole. I always feel one asks for trouble by saying a course seems alright, although going to the other extreme is almost as bad. I prefer to say nothing – until I pass the finishing post on the second day. The steeplechase course seemed to present no special problems, but it was somewhat twisty, and would need to be ridden with a clear head.

Gillian, Kit and I led the rest of the competitors round the course at a good pace, and we heard one of the officials ask whether the English women rode as fast as they walked.

Wild Venture was the first horse in the dressage arena next morning. It had poured with rain intermittently over Denmark for the past month, and overnight there was yet another deluge which made conditions extremely difficult. During Venture's test the heavens opened again, and although the weather brightened later in the day, it was too late to make any improvement. Our second British pair were Gillian and Willie, and then it was Chips' turn.

Never have I seen a dressage arena in a worse state. The corners were a quagmire, and wherever the horses had been, there were deep tracks. I did not realise exactly how bad it was until after we had saluted the judges and moved off at a walk to start the test. At the bottom of the arena I saw the muddy, black patches, but it was too late to cut the corner without throwing Chips off balance, and thereby losing valuable marks, so I just walked steadfastly forward, hoping for the best. Unfortunately, Chips objected strongly to such going in an arena where he obviously expected velvety conditions, and in a second, he had shied away to the inside. A few marks were lost. Then came another calamity; we had just finished a movement involving very tight half-circles and were supposed to go on into an extended trot. I all but took the wrong course and was only just in time to give Chips the correct aids for extension. To make matters worse the same thing happened as we came to the end of the test, but this time it was not quite as noticeable. He had done the 'see-saw', and moved off into a canter perfectly – this was the movement which had caused us so much trouble at Harewood. In a few strides we should have walked, but I was about to canter blithely on, and again had to do some quick thinking to save an error of course, and I was terribly worried, but luckily Chips had otherwise performed very well, and when all the marks were announced at the end of the day, we stood in second place by eight marks. The German horse, Franco, ridden by Lutke Westhues, was ahead of Chips in the individual placings, while Germany and Sweden led Britain as Teams. Our prospects looked somewhat dismal and the reports of our showing in the papers next morning did nothing to raise our spirits. It seemed as if we were to be the team to break the winning British tradition.

At ten-minute intervals, we set off on the one and a half hour endurance test, and so by the time Chips and I started along the roads and tracks of phase A, Venture had already finished the course. At the time I had no idea of how he had fared except that over the steeplechase course he had obtained maximum bonus marks. Gillian and Willie were somewhere on the course, miles ahead of me. Phase A was soon finished, and we set off at a fast gallop towards the first steeplechase fence. The course was on the Copenhagen racetrack and eleven fences were to be jumped in two and a half miles. Chips flew over them all easily and was still going strongly as we passed the finishing post. He regained his breath even before we reached the first kilometre marker of the second roads and tracks, and this delighted me for I knew then that he must, after all, be very fit. My personal time checks at the various kilometre markers were all slightly in advance, so I slowed Chips to a walk until the extra minutes sped by. Then off we trotted again, and eventually arrived at the end of C with six minutes in hand.

Chips was sponged down, and Bob Armstrong, the British farrier, screwed studs into his hind shoes. Colonel Weldon was there to see each member of the Team off on the cross-country phase and knew exactly what had befallen both Venture and Willie. He was about to tell me of the trouble there had been, and to advise me accordingly, but I implored him not to. At all these Trials I carried a picture of the course in my mind; of where I intend to go, and where to jump, and to hear of trouble or disaster at any particular fence was, to me, absolutely fatal. I simply had to be allowed to ride the course as I had planned. This might seem rather silly to some people, but it was just a personal foible of mine, and neither my mother nor father would ever have dreamed of telling me anything of the grief that there had been. The fact that I hadn't wanted Weldon to tell me what had befallen others did not please him, and probably contributed to the myth that I was not a good team member.

The six minutes were up, and we came under starter's orders. Five, four, three, two, one and then we were off and galloping towards the first fence. Someone once said that Chips and I have only one pace – flat out – and they were quite right. We reached top gear in a few hundred yards and stayed in it until the end of the course. Unless something goes wrong. Over the first post-and-rails we flew and in the next minute we were at the second fence with its nasty slide. Chips slipped, coming into it, but recovered in time to hop over the rails, slithered down to the bottom of the slide and up again to leap the third rails. We landed with a thump over the drop and turned almost on two legs towards the next obstacle. Then we were nearing the 'pedestrian crossing' with its muddy approach, but Chips made nothing of it and galloped on strongly until we reached number nine.

This was a straightforward pile of logs, and we met it quite wrong. Chips stood off yards from it, and I felt him really stretch himself in the effort of clearing it. He must have leapt the most tremendous width. It was after this fence that I made my mistake. The track to number ten was deep with mud, and I had already decided to swing left under the trees to avoid this. Unfortunately, there were many low branches and I had to crouch low on Chips' neck and shut my eyes. He, too, must have been going with his eyes shut, for when I turned him at the last minute to the fence, he stopped dead. I was more than surprised but collected myself quickly for a second attempt and this time he went straight over. I can only think that I unsighted him completely in the first place by coming out from the trees at too short a distance from the fence.

As we negotiated the other two parts of it, I was muttering away, furious with myself for allowing such a thing to happen when there were so many more hazards to come. Fences fifteen and sixteen, the bank combination with rails proved no difficulty to us, and neither did the huge open ditch and rails, where Chips seemed hardly to exert himself before we landed safely on the far side. Then we were in and out of the farm yard, over the garden seat and making for the next fence in a straight line.

The line I was taking ran over the edge of a golf course and across one of the greens. It would have saved me precious seconds, and so I had steeled myself against a natural hesitance at cutting up the green. However, someone had foreseen the possibility of this happening and taken steps to prevent it. At the last minute I saw that the whole green was roped off. Frantically I pulled Chips around. We skidded along the rope, and almost fell over in the effort of negotiating the turn to get back onto the directed track. Instead of gaining time, I had lost it, and was again very annoyed with myself.

Soon the ravine fences were ahead of us. We leapt the first element without any trouble, went down the slide and jumped the trakehner and ditch, then we bounded up the far side and hopped neatly over the rails at the top. My anticipated horror fence was the next. I really drove Chips hard as we approached the big drop guarded by the garden fencing, but he was utterly unperturbed and we merely stepped over it and had landed in the roadway almost before I realised it. On we galloped until the penultimate fence was only a few strides away. Chips jumped the triple rails neatly and we landed with a tremendous splash in the water. Another stride and we were in the deep part and then up on to the hump of an island and down again at its other side. Deep water again and only one stride in the shallows before leaping the last fence.

The cross-country was over but we had still to do the run in, and then the whole speed and endurance test was finished. Peter Scott-Dunne, the British veterinary surgeon and Pat, Chips' groom attended to his needs while I was bundled into a waiting Land Rover and driven back to the start of the cross-country, there to be asked by Colonel Weldon whether I could pass on any useful information as to how the course had ridden. However, apart from what I had learnt from my mistake at the tenth fence there was nothing I could say, so eventually, I went back to find Chips had already left for the stables and Peter Scott-Dunne was waiting for the next British pair.

By the end of the day we were all finished safely, although Gillian had had two nasty falls off Just William. Venture, Chips and Cat had all stopped once at different places, but little Laurien had gone round clear. In spite of his refusal though, Chips still returned the fastest time of the day, and was the best performer over the course. His bonus score more than trebled his penalties. The German horse, Franco, also went clear round the course, but was not nearly as fast. Chips and I accordingly pulled up another point, so were then only seven behind for Individual honours. Everything depended on the show jumping phase the next day. The British Team had moved up from its third place to second, above Sweden.

In the morning we were all up at first light to go to the stables at Charlottenlund and run up each horse in hand. Not one of them was unlevel, two were a little stiff, but no more than one would expect after such a marathon the day before. At the official veterinary inspection, they were all passed sound. Chips was looking around at the crowd with great interest and I was hoping he would start thinking of our responsibilities in the afternoon's final show jumping. The

German Team horses were also sound, but some of the other horses were extremely dispirited and clearly still very tired.

The rain was still falling in unceasing torrents and showed no signs of abating. It was far from pleasant, and I felt even less comfortable when I saw the state of the jumping ground. It was terribly slippery and muddy. Not at all the sort of conditions I would choose at a time when so much depended on this jumping. However, I consoled myself with the fact that it was the same for everybody and hoped that all would go well for Chips and me and the rest of the British Team.

Queen Ingrid was present at the trials, and when Chips turn came, we cantered in and saluted before the Royal Box. The bell rang and off we went towards the first fences. The fourth one was a difficult obstacle – a combination over banks, involving a very quick turn on landing up on the first one, and then a jump down over poles to ground level again. I had anticipated trouble there, but Chips jumped it perfectly and went on over number five, a hog's back over water, number six, and number seven, a brilliantly coloured wall. The eighth fence was a garden gate, complete with border plants, and coming into this Chips slipped and lost his rhythm and impetus. He cleared the gate but at the water dropped a foot – ten faults. The tenth fence was another combination, one of cross-country proportions and somewhat reminiscent of the 'silage pit' at the Harewood Trials. We jumped into the dip over some rails, then had to negotiate a big parallel bars with water before emerging out of the dip over more rails. Everyone seemed to have made mistakes there, but Chips managed to clear all three parts. I was busy congratulating him when we met the next one all wrong, and down it went. Twenty penalties altogether, and although we had no more, I was quite convinced that, with such a score, any chance we might have had for challenging Franco was gone forever. Meanwhile the Team placings were also in the balance, and not until Laurien jumped the only clear round of the day did we realise the award was safe for Britain.

Franco came into the ring, and I rushed to the rails to watch his round. He started well and seemed to be jumping safely. I despaired of his hitting even a single fence, but then, at number five, he was careless, and a rail fell from the hog's back. The garden-gate was right in front of me, and that, too, fell from its supports. Twenty penalties, and I knew that if he hit another, Chips would go into the lead. I watched him jump clear into the 'silage pit' fence, and saw him emerge over the third element. The second part was hidden from sight. Then he negotiated the last two fences and cantered towards the exit. I was sure he had had only two fences down and ran up to congratulate Lutke Westhues on what I thought was victory. At that time, I imagined he looked at me rather strangely, and a moment or so later I realised why. He had hit the middle part of the pit fence, so Chips and I moved up to first Individual place, only three points ahead of our erstwhile leader. No one could have been more sportsmanlike in accepting last-minute defeat than my German rival, for as soon as the results were announced he became one of the first to say, 'Well done'.

For the last time I rode Chips into the arena, and he stood to attention while the Union Jack unfurled, and our National Anthem was played. Queen Ingrid presented me with her own trophy; I was given a sash of honour for being Individual winner and another as a member of the leading Team. Chips was not forgotten, for he was presented with a garland of carrots made in the shape of a horseshoe; so, during the following ceremonies, he behaved perfectly, content to munch at the carrots I plucked from round his neck.

The European Trials at Copenhagen were over at last. All the spectators began to drift away in the dusk, and Chips and I returned to the stables along roads reflecting the lights on their wet surfaces. In a final farewell that evening competitors and officials gathered at a gigantic banquet, and we listened to speeches from the organisers and several visitors. There were toasts to be drunk, and at last we raised our glasses for the last time. The toast was 'The Horse, and a particular horse – High and Mighty'. Hundreds of guests stood to drink to him, to Chip, who had really shown the world his worth. No horse was ever more aptly name – High and Mighty.

Scrambling over the tenth fence at Copenhagen. Strange to say, we landed quite safely.

The eleventh fence a few yards away, jumping in our old style.

Eyes screwed up and mouth open as we rise from deep water to take the thirty-fourth, and last fence.

Chapter Nineteen – My Broken Heart

After Copenhagen, we picked up the autumn programme. We went to Harringay for the Horse of the Year Show where for the second year in succession, we won the combined training class with its dressage test followed by a round of show jumps. Then we went to the Tweseldown One-Day Event and we won there. On to Chatsworth during the third week of October, and the weather was awful. We were a very bedraggled bunch on the Official Walk Round, led by Colonel Babe Moseley. Little rivulets were already forming all over the steep hillside on the first half of the course and the Ice Pond was growing wider and deeper as the day progressed. We would need the longest square studs in Chips' shoes to get a better grip on the ground which was going to be extremely slippery on the following day.

In the dressage Chips managed to ignore the weather and we produced a very good test with 93.67 marks, with Margaret Hough on Bambi 14.55 behind, and Laurien snapping at her heels, 0.67 points further back. In the show jumping I was too careful and was penalised 1.5 marks on time and 10 more for one fence down. Laurien moved up to only 3.83 behind me.

In the afternoon the weather cheered up and the crowds were now out in force. Chips and I sailed round the course. Laurien dashed down the hillside to the Ice Pond, and just as she was taking off her hind legs slipped forward, nearer to the fence. Impetus was suddenly lost. Her forehand went forty-five degrees into the air and then came straight down to land safely in the pond. Derek's legs had gone backwards towards her tail as this happened and his weight at this angle on the stirrups and their leathers meant that they slipped straight out of the steel keepers in the saddle. One stirrup immediately disappeared into the water below. The other hung, precariously, upside down on his foot. He tried to lean over and grab the trailing leather as Laurien and he stood in the Pond but to no avail. Clearly, he had decided he was not going to carry on without them, and to the crowd's amusement, he jumped off and frantically started to fish in the ice-cold water to find them. Once he had them he secured them back on to the saddle and climbed aboard. Laurien, meanwhile, had enjoyed a quiet rest. Had Derek forgotten that by dismounting he had incurred 60 penalties – the equivalent of a fall! He also lost a further

60 points on fishing time. There was a considerable amount of other grief over the wet course and, at the end of the day, Chips had won the Chatsworth Event for the second year running by 82.4 marks. In The Times they wrote: "That amazing pair, Miss Sheila Willcox and High and Mighty, set the seal on a fine season by yet another clear cut victory. Even compared with our best horsemen and horses, they stand alone, a remarkable combination achieved by strenuous and patient work and an opportunism that amounts to genius."

Chips and I had won seven out of eight British Events in which we had taken part and been third in the eighth (the Cottesbrooke disaster). The only other event open to us had been the Harewood Three-Day Event when we had had to compete *hors concours.* Chips had gone back out to his field for a well-earned rest and I visited him once a day with his bucket of oats. He was always looking out for me and whinnied a welcome and cantered to the gate. I settled down and finished the original *Three Days Running*, without a mention of my illicit love affair with Ted Marsh, and skirting tactfully around the issues with Frank Weldon and the way they had purloined Chips and utterly failed with him. It was published in April 1958 and sold out on the first day and was serialised by The Daily Post.

A week after Chatsworth I attended the Annual Eventing Conference at the Russell Hotel. Chips had won the Calcutta Cup for the most successful event horse for the second year running, and I had won the Tony Collings Memorial trophy, also for a second time. I was astonished when Derek Allhussen seconded by John Oram, suggested that the dressage test should now be given back more influence. When the British were abroad there was still the original percentages of marks, and perhaps they had realised just how important dressage was in terms of training for the horses during the jumping.

Yevonde, the society photographer took more shots of me, this time in a pretty dress, a head and shoulders that adorned the society page in *Country Life* at the end of October. I was asked to write forewords for books and went to Northern Ireland for the Sportsman's Ball at the Orpheus Ballroom in Belfast where I was the Guest of Honour and asked to make a speech.

Ted and I continued to meet at Dunsley and in London. We were both sure that eventually we would receive a dispensation from the

Catholic church and would be able to marry. Meanwhile we made love at every opportunity.

In November, I was interviewed by Barbara Cooper who came up to Lytham on behalf of the magazine, *Illustrated*. She wanted to run a series of three articles supported by specially taken photographs. The first of these was to be 'the non-horsey Sheila, enjoying London's night life'. I could see a problem here, the only man in my life was Ted and obviously we could not publicly flaunt our relationship. I cast around for a suitable male partner and could only come up with one eventing acquaintance who was extremely good looking but happily paired up with his girlfriend. Perhaps at this point, alarm bells should have been ringing in my ears. I was so tied up with an old married man that I wasn't out having fun with my social peers.

The handsome young man, John Andrews, agreed to be photographed with me after his girlfriend had been consulted. Next, I was invited to attend the Martini Rossi Awards at the Hyde Park Hotel for the presentation of the leading Horsewoman of the Year. It was won by Pat Smythe, as she had a huge following in the very popular sport of show jumping. To my surprise I was runner-up. I made a speech saying that I was looking for a younger horse to bring on.

This resulted in a letter from Mrs Vivian Eason asking if I might be interested in a home-bred five-year-old, Cresta Run. Vivian and Ted had bred him with a good quality mare to a Premium stallion. I decided that his competition name would be Airs and Graces. I made good friends with Vivian and Ted and loved the area they lived in, the Cotswolds.

In private, back at home, I became more and more worried. I was always so regular and I had not had my period. I told Ted but he merely placated me, telling me not to worry. He and I had already discussed children and he had said he didn't want anymore, he wanted me all to himself. Mummy noticed my state of mind and confronted me. I admitted that I thought I might be pregnant and she immediately guessed it was Ted. When I confirmed this, she was horrified and retorted that I had been so stupid, a man like that would just use me and then discard me. I told her this wasn't true and explained how we hoped we could marry and his secretary was in contact with the Vatican seeking a dispensation. She told me in no uncertain terms that was never going to happen. He hadn't even done anything to actually get a divorce. She believed that he was merely stringing me along.

Suddenly God looked down and I got my period, I wasn't pregnant! I was so upset by this episode that I was persuaded by Mummy and Daddy that I mustn't see Ted anymore. I complied. In many ways I was still a child, living at home, and trying to please my parents.

Life went on and I was raw. I had to force myself to shut Ted out of my mind and concentrate on the new horse, Cresta. I could not allow myself to fall to pieces. I had made my choice, I chose the Catholic church and in reality, my parents' approbation, rather than Ted. Looking back, I wished that I had stuck to the original plan and waited for Ted's divorce and married him. I would have had a husband who shared my interest in horses and all the facilities to train horses that one could ever wish for. I believed that Ted would always have been faithful to me. I didn't have the maturity and understanding that a twenty-something year old girl would have these days, that if a man is unfaithful to his first wife then undoubtedly, he would be unfaithful to his next.

Mummy was desperately ringing around, trying to find a suitable male for me who was Catholic. In the meantime, I received an invitation from the Queen on a large oblong card headed with the gold crown and underneath E I I R also in raised gold. It said:

THE LORD CHAMBERLAIN is commanded by HER MAJESTY
to summon Miss Sheila Willcox
to an Afternoon Presentation Party at Buckingham Palace
on Wednesday, the 19th March, 1958
from 3.30 to 5.30 o'clock p.m.
Ladies: Day Dress with Hat.
Gentlemen: Morning Dress; Non-Ceremonial Day Dress.
If in possession Swords should be worn.

I thought the bit about the sword absolutely splendid, and only wished that I had a sword to wear. This new dress code was a big departure from the past, when there had been a time-honoured tradition of the Presentation of Debutantes at seventeen years of age, daughters from all the smart families in the country who, until this year had had a Buckingham Palace party for themselves alone and who had appeared before their Queen and the Duke of Edinburgh in elegant long dresses with high feathers in their hair. The Palace had decided that they needed to change their image and had adopted a more eclectic style and added more 'ordinary' people to the list. Lady Allardyce, the mother of Stewart Goodfellow had been responsible for my invitation.

Mummy immediately began to worry about my outfit, particularly the hat. Eventually I dressed in a light grey chiffon frock with the tiniest hat stuck on the back of my head. Lady Allardyce accompanied me and we arrived by taxi at the steps leading up into the Palace and waited around for a very long time, during which I caught several curious glances from the debutantes who were clearly puzzled as to why I was there. Eventually, we entered the throne room and when my name was called, I had to walk up to the dais on which the Queen and Prince Philip sat and made a low curtsy which I had been practising religiously. They both smiled at me in response. I backed away the number of required steps and then turned around and went back in line. It crossed my mind that it must be very boring for the Queen, and also for the Prince. It was a great honour, but I had to hurry home to Lytham. The horses were waiting for me, there were only two weeks before the start of the season.

In the background Mummy was still searching for a suitable husband for me, like a mother out of Jane Austen times. She produced a Catholic bachelor in the form of Busty Kevill, who was prepared to ask me to be his partner for the evening at the Holcombe Hunt's Ball which took place at Hoghton Tower, the family resident of the ancient line of the de Hoghtons. Busty, at that point was about forty years old and time was running out if he was to produce children to inherit his family inheritance. He wanted to continue on the line with the Kevill surname. He wanted children quickly, but Mummy carefully didn't mention this. So Busty and I went to the ball, he even asked me out to dinner a week before so we could get to know each other. I must have been in a black mood, although I tried to be light-hearted, I found this whole exercise extremely depressing. I knew I had to move on as surely as Ted already had.

Busty telephoned me to say that we had been asked by Lady de Hoghton to join their private party for dinner before the Hunt Ball began at their house. I perked up, perhaps this might be rather fun. I knew that Lady de Hoghton was Sir Cuthbert's second wife and very much younger than he was. The de Hoghton family tree went back to Saxon times when a Saxon heiress had married a Norman knight, whose liege lord was William the Conqueror and the couple had settled at Hoghton Tower. The house is set seven hundred feet above sea level, and the name 'de Hoghton' means 'of the high hill'. I had to have a dress that was suitable for a visit to such an ancient and noble house.

When I had still been seeing Ted, I saw an absolutely beautiful dress in a shop in Bond Street, three-quarter length, pale pink, off the shoulder moulded to the figure but widening into a swaying bell of a skirt. I tried it on and it looked enchanting, but it cost £20 which I could not afford. I told Ted about it and he bought it for me. When I wore it, I felt like a million dollars and this was to be my outfit for Hoghton Tower.

After dinner the ladies retired to touch up their makeup and went back to join the men for coffee. I walked in and felt someone staring at me. It was a very attractive young man, one hand resting laconically on the mantle shelf with its hot flames spiralling up the chimney. He was gazing at me in a manner I had never seen before – intent, covetous. My heart lurched in response.

Later in the evening he approached me and said, "I am John Waddington. Who are you?". I told him and so began our love affair. Poor Busty returned to find us deep in conversation, but we were oblivious to everyone else. John and I danced together. All the dancing was in ballroom style, the waltz, quickstep and tango. John had been taught to dance beautifully. He had perfected the knack of leading with the top of his leg so far forward that it went well between my legs and I could feel his very hard erection every other step. This was extremely disconcerting, but it was very satisfying to be the cause of such male excitement. I don't know how I got home that night, I was in a daze.

The next day the telephone rang, "John Waddington," he announced himself. He wanted to take me out to dinner. Then began a persistent courtship which must have thrilled my mother. There was no doubt that he was totally besotted with me and I became equally enamoured of him. He dressed well and was never to be seen in public, without a perfectly pressed crease down his trousers and highly polished shoes. His manners were impeccable. He was tall, broad, and his strong legs had curvy calves which made me laugh. He was inclined to be a little pompous, but I found this amusing and loved to laugh at him.

On paper John was everything I could wish for. Although, I had found young men my own age a little gauche and immature, John Waddington was different. He had an air of sophistication and social graces in abundance. He was twenty-two years old, the same age as myself. He had spent two years of national service in London as a Coldstreamer in the Brigade of Guards.

He had an air of assurance and was the elder son of the owners of several mills in the Rossendale Valley. His suits were well-cut made by the 'right' tailor, his parents had given him a permanent suite at the Grosvenor Hotel and he knew his way about London nightlife, the 'right' restaurants and nightclubs. His grandfather had made the family fortune with the mills and had then become the local MP. So, although I was not exactly the 'right class' we were at least both northerners. I was enjoying a great deal of social cachet through the publicity generated by my successful eventing career, so I might have appeared to be a glittering prize. On the surface, we made a handsome couple.

When I met John the mills were still doing well. John's mother had originally been a beautiful dark-haired local girl but when she married into the Waddington family she transformed herself into a lady of the manor. Third generation John was the handsome, favourite son who was in line to take over the mills. He worked hard in the factory and was knowledgeable about the family business.

While our love affair was developing, I felt a traitor to Ted. I couldn't understand how I could fall in love with John when a part of me would always belong to Ted. Later John told me that when he had seen me coming through those doors at Hoghton Tower on Busty's arm, he had just stared at me, and had said to himself, "That's the one for me!" This was the beginning of his eager and passionate pursuit.

He was courting me, picking me up every evening in his sporty silver Sunbeam Talbot. In those days there was nowhere to make love except in his car, and although it was fitted with the latest reclining seats, it required great dexterity to move about and produced purple bruises in all sorts of places from the gear stick. It was impossible for us to have really satisfying sex in the car because once I had managed to get into place straddling him, I would hit my head on the roof.

I was invited to a weekend party with one of John's ex-girlfriends who was now married. He flirted outrageously to make me jealous and annoy her husband. He succeeded on both counts and was not very popular. Then doubts began to creep in. John must have seen the danger signals and immediately began to woo me again and I was persuaded that we were meant to be together. He invited me for dinner at the Imperial Hotel in Blackpool and I dressed up.

We arrived at the hotel and made our way into the foyer to sit down. Immediately a waiter was beside John. He ordered champagne cocktails, which arrived as if someone had been standing at the ready. I had been teetotal until he introduced me to one of these in the early days of our courtship and I had been surprised by how much I enjoyed it. I still abhorred gin and brandy and all the other cocktails, but I had a weakness for the champagne variety. Just one put me in a rosy glow and I became somewhat weak around the knees. We sipped at our drinks and then he reached into his pocket and drew out a little box. I realised what was coming. He said, "Will you marry me?" For an instant Ted flickered across my vision and I dismissed him. I believed that I had fallen in love with John and he was obviously in love with me.

I said yes, and he slipped the most beautiful diamond ring onto my wedding finger. The Head Waiter appeared with two more champagne cocktails. Following the strict code of propriety John asked my parents if he might call one evening to see Daddy and ask formally for my hand. Although John was not a Catholic, he was at least the right age and single, and Mummy had managed perfectly well with Daddy not being a Catholic. Daddy found his attitude a little supercilious, but I assured him that underneath he was a nice person and didn't mean offence.

Mummy and Daddy agreed that John would take my hand in marriage. The announcement would be made in the Daily Telegraph on 12th April 1958. I was dreading telling Ted, but it had to be done before the news was made public. This was one of the hardest things I had ever had to do. I rang him and told him and there was a dead silence on the other end of the line. Then, in a distant voice he said, "I hope you will be very happy." I begged him to come to the wedding and he promised that he would.

The Press received the announcement of our engagement with great enthusiasm, but I was already off on the trials circuit with Chips and my young horse Cresta. He had a good temperament and I worked on his dressage until he was sufficiently obedient then I began his jump training. It began with poles on the ground and then progressed to show jumps. We encountered a problem with this as he continually knocked down the top pole, no matter how perfectly I presented him on the correct stride.

I devised a system of rapping him that involved a string pulley so that as he went over the jump I would pull the string and the pole would go up and hit him on the legs between his hoofs and his fetlock joints. It didn't really work as by the time the pole lifted it was too late.

I had to think of another way to cure him of this problem. I taught him to jump down a line of coloured show jumping poles set at an easy two feet in height, where he had to bounce, land and take off immediately. He had to learn how to round his back and use his hind legs. Whenever he jumped clear I made a great fuss of him, telling him how clever he was. As soon as I heard him clip the top pole with his hoof, I growled at him.

He would never be a natural jumper, as Chips was and sometimes the photographs showed him looking like a swan in distress in the air above the jump. I entered him for his first one-day event at Glanusk and he competed in the preliminary class, Chips was entered in the open. Both horses had gone through their twelve-week training programme, so they were fit enough. Daddy arranged that I go and stay with his old friends Cherry and Sidney Harris near Henley-in-Arden for a few days before the event, so we could really concentrate on our work.

Cresta, called Airs and Graces, did well at Glanusk and was beaten into second place three marks behind Claude Allhusen (Derek's wife). This was a good beginning. Chips produced an immaculate dressage test and then went on into first place with a winning margin of 28.3 points. At Stowell I was too confident of an easy victory, beating Derek Allhusen and Ted, but then Chips sensing my lack of attention put in a dirty stop at an easy stone wall. This refusal closed the gap between the three of us and I won by only 1.1 marks. Ted was third on Wild Venture, closely followed by Blue Jeans. Badminton was on in just under two weeks.

We moved to Bourton Far Hill to stay with the Easons, and I continued to train the horses. The Duke and Duchess of Beaufort gave a drinks party for all the competitors and their close relations in one of the large reception rooms at Badminton House. This year the Queen and the Queen Mother were house guests of the Duke and they were also attending the party. This meant that all ladies had to wear gloves and dress was formal, smart frocks for ladies and best suits for men. My parents had been invited and also John, as my fiancé.

At the party, the Queen made her way towards us, John in his best double-breasted suit and me in a blue velvet three-quarter length frock. She congratulated us on our engagement. Afterwards John and I drove back to our hotel in his dark blue Jaguar sports car and it was almost like Princess Diana, with the press in pursuit of us. We ended up evading them and climbed through a kitchen window into the hotel as they were waiting outside for us. In the end Daddy persuaded us that it would be easier to let the Press in and they took photos of me sitting in an armchair with John perched on one of its arms. After that they left us in peace.

There were 88 entries at Badminton that year, but some had not completed the entrance requirements and couldn't start. This included Colonel Weldon's young six-year-old horse, Fermoy. Ultimately there were 60 starters, which meant that the dressage would take two days. At this point women were still banned from competing in the Olympics Three-Day Event and this was mentioned a great deal by the press who were pointing out how well Chips and I went, beating the men again and again. They pointed out the illogicality that women could compete in the European Championships but not in the upcoming 1960 Olympic Games in Rome.

Chips and I were not competing until the second dressage day. We all walked the cross-country course and it was a great deal more difficult than the year before. It was being run in reverse order, so going the other way, we ran into some difficult fences early on. There was a great deal of discussion over the new fences, the difference in the Quarry where we would approach from the opposite direction and jump downhill over number 6, stiff rails with a big drop, then go up the other side to emerge by jumping number 7, more uninviting Rails. We then had to turn sharply to the left, jump a 3 feet 9 inch Spruce fence and turn again to negotiate a second big drop approached by another right-angled turn. It would require a listening and co-operative horse to get through this maze quickly, without losing balance and speed.

Soon after that we were faced with a very difficult fence in Huntsman's Close, a square dug dry ditch, very wide and spooky, hidden on the approach by the ground having been made up into the shape of a hump with sloping sides. Over the first hump in the ground the horse would be taken entirely by surprise as this wide ditch opened beneath his feet, and in the middle of it was set a single, airy horizontal rail with five supporting uprights. At the far side of the ditch, on landing had been built a replica of the first grassy hump.

There were two alternatives of attack. The first was to be brave, come in so fast that Chips would have no chance to see the ditch until, hopefully, it was too late for him to stop, as there would be problems if he did do that. The second possibility was to come in on a short and bouncy stride, take one stride towards the top of the hump, over it and then 'hop' across the ditch, and it would be a big wide hop! And repeat the method dealing with the hump as we landed on the far side to be on our way. The first alternative would need very strong riding and considerable pace to fly safely from the top of one hump to the other. The second would rely on the horse being prepared to hop without hesitation. I would need to make a decision during a solitary return visit with undisturbed deep thought and much running about pretending to be Chips for each of my two alternatives in an effort to see what it would look like to him. I decided I could not count on Chips hopping across without thinking it too dangerous, and I opted to try coming in at speed and giving him no time to think twice before he was in the air.

On Friday morning I was getting ready for our dressage test. Pat Robson, who was acting as groom, and I made him look like the million dollars I thought he was worth and he emerged from his stable with his mane beautifully plaited, tail picked out laboriously by hand, strand by strand, to make it look as full as possible. His coat glowed with good health and his eyes were bright with anticipation.

We went through the intricate movements of the dressage test and the steward gave me a broad grin as I exited through the gap. He said quietly, "Jolly well done!" as we passed him and I grinned back and said, "Thank you." As Chips emerged into the surrounding ring, there was an immediate burst of loud and prolonged applause and I showed the crowd my appreciation by smiling and patting Chips' neck and telling him what a terrific horse he was. He was a horse in a million and I loved him. We were a real partnership. We scored 37 penalties, which was the lowest penalty score ever achieved in this phase at Badminton. We would go into the second phase with a long lead of 22 penalties.

I was feeling very confident on the morning of the speed and endurance phase, and enjoyed my breakfast of bacon, two eggs, toast and marmalade and coffee. I checked on Chips and then went off again to inspect the Quarry fences, and finally made the decision to come in at speed and fly it. As the morning progressed the tension was rising. The weather was cool and I was looking forward to our round. As we rode towards the start, we had to go past the grandstand and close to the cross-country course. There was lots of noise and masses of people walking about from fence to fence. This excited the horses and wound them up even before they began.

My parents and John were watching us gallop twice around the circuit and I had a marvellous feeling, sailing over the steeplechase fences and the big open ditch, jumping out of our stride, with the cold air bringing blood to my cheeks. I knew that if we maintained this speed, we would earn bonus points. Round the roads and tracks and Chips was passed sound. Then we had a few minutes rest and we were off on the cross-country.

In no time we were approaching the first difficult group of fences at the Quarry. Coming in to the big drop, it looked as if there was nowhere to land, but Chips knew what was there and just 'popped' it in the most economical way. We were up the other side, out over the rails at the top, turned left sharply but still in balance with me warning Chips there was a jump immediately. Over that and a very quick right to jump over a second big drop. So far, so good.

As we were within three strides of the first hump, I put my foot down on the accelerator and he shot forward. I felt a slight quiver as he saw what was there, but it was too late for him to do anything but rise in the air, and then we landed safely on the other side. Three more fences and we approached the turn into the Coffin, which required spot on accuracy on the take-off, one short rounded stride downhill with me sitting very tight, leaning slightly forward, but ready to pick up his forehand if he stumbled. I asked him to jump strongly across the ditch, then a big push with me leaning forward to encourage him again, for a decisive uphill stride, and a clean jump out on to the flat ground again.

We continued on around the course, Chips obeying every nuanced command until we came to the brushwood with the ditch in front. As he took off, I felt the slightest delay and on landing he seemed to lose some of his innate fluency and I gave him a sharp admonitory tap on his neck to warn him to be more careful and we turned right on to our line for the big spread of the Vicarage Ditch. I drove him into it, allowing him no room for moving off our line, and he cleared it. At that point he was back to his normal, good mode and I wondered if I had imagined that something was not as it should be. We settled into his usual consuming gallop, jumped the difficult number 27 with consummate ease and set sail for the big Bullfinch. Then there were only four more fences and we focused on a specific point to jump into the lake, turn in the air to land in the shallow water only one stride up onto the bank and through the finish into the run in. We had gone clear and I learnt that we had gained maximum bonus points of 37.6 on the steeplechase and only 3.2 below the maximum on the cross-country, so our score was 77.6.

Then I realised that he had lost his off-fore shoe, so no wonder he had been a bit out of sorts at the Vicarage Ditch with the big spread. It wasn't his bad mood but something rather serious going wrong. When the last competitors' marks went up, I saw that we were now 52.13 marks ahead! I imagined that John was very proud to have picked the winner!

There were 57 starters for yesterday's speed and endurance test as there were 17 eliminations. Two more were withdrawn before the veterinary inspection. Chips passed the vet. In the show jumping we could afford to knock down five fences to be challenged by second placed Anneli Drummond-Hay on Pluto. Chips could go lame, absolutely refuse to jump, or knock everything down. Nothing is ever a sure thing with horses!

This is what was reported in *Country Life*: "When High and Mighty entered the ring towards the end of the show jumping phase, he was greeted with considerable interest, and although he could have walked light heartedly through five of the 12 obstacles and still been the victor, something special is always expected of him. Determined to provide the anticipatory thrill, he hit an early fence but jumped in fine style until, with a remarkable sense of theatre which brought forth gasps of amazement he seemed to stop at the last fence when almost in mid-air and then cleared it very efficiently with the minimum of disturbance to Miss Willcox's excellent seat. He had only ten faults."

We had won again, and the crowd erupted into loud applause. I was not at all sure that we deserved such largesse after one fence down and another Houdini spectacular but at least no one could say that Chips was boring! Our final score was plus 68.02 and we won by 47 marks from Derek Allhusen and Laurien with Anneli Drummond-Hay third on Pluto.

The photographer for the magazine *Light Horse* snapped a picture of us just before we went into the dressage arena, Chips looking calmly interested, I sitting deep in the saddle biting my lip in concentration. The caption was: "Art and nature thus allied, go to make a – "pretty ride", and in due course a "pretty bride", too. Sheila Willcox celebrated her engagement to John Waddington by a most polished dressage performance on High and Mighty and a decisive second victory at Badminton."

There was an urgent call for us to go to be interviewed again for the BBC by Dorian Williams who had no problem last year about where in Lancashire the Willcoxes lived. This year his memory failed him, and he solemnly told viewers before our interview that Sheila Willcox had trained High and Mighty on the sands of St Helens! The Lancastrians among the viewers must have fallen off their chairs laughing at even the thought of this. St Helens might be a fine town to the good people who lived there, but it was close to Liverpool and was surrounded by industrial Lancashire with not a beach in sight. Many of the locals from St Annes and Lytham bombarded the BBC switchboard to complain bitterly. I was in awe of my wonderful horse and all he had achieved. Badminton was going to be, forever, a very special place for us. We returned home to a great welcome.

Soon afterwards I was in huge demand for book signings, dressage displays, and programmes such as Woman's Hour. I was asked to open the Stanley Matthews Exhibition of Sport at Olympia in Blackpool. I met other famous sportspeople such as Stanley Matthews, at that time England's finest footballer; Brian London, British heavy weight boxing champion; Alfred Gregory, the Everest climber; and Reg Harris, the champion racing cyclist.

John and I were trying to decide where we would live. He worked each day at the mill at Haslingden so we started looking within a radius of 15 miles. We had to take into consideration that I would be bringing with me two horses and neither of us doubted that I would be continuing to ride and for that I needed countryside.

As well as this issue I had other things to consider. Despite my successes it appeared that the Olympic committee were still determined that eventing was open only to men. So, it looked like my dream of winning Olympic gold on Chips would never come true. He was now eleven years old. After a great deal of thought I decided that there was really no point in competing further with Chips in anything. He had won all the prizes open to him and no horse would ever again give me as much pleasure and success.

Then I was struck with the thought that originally Chips had been bred for hunting. Now he would be a dream hunter. I decided to offer him to Ted. I wrote to him explaining my wish and he rang me to say he would love to have Chips and when he was too old to continue hunting he would return him to me. I did have one instruction, he was to 'go with' Chips over the fences, and not to use his old-fashioned backward seat. He promised to try. I wasn't sure how I had come up with such a plan. I knew that Ted had been terribly hurt when I had announced my engagement, and I reasoned that, in a strange way, I was trying to make it up to him. Perhaps I couldn't quite sever our connection, and this was a way of staying in contact.

The autumn event season opened, and I took Cresta to Melton Mowbray competing in the intermediate class. He hit a narrow stile around the cross-country and we fell but I was picked up and put back on him and he seemed to have learnt from his mistake and picked his feet up properly. Shortly after this was Harewood Three-Day Event which would be a big test and a considerable challenge for my novice horse.

We rode a good dressage test and took the lead until the very last competitor rode into the arena. It was the German, Otto Pohlmann riding Polarfuchs who had won several three-day events in Germany. Until I came along, the Germans alone were renowned for their dressage prowess, both in Grand Prix dressage and particularly in the dressage part of a three-day event. On this day Polarfuchs produced a very smooth and pleasing test and he took over the lead with 18.33 penalty points, now only 1.34 marks separated the two of us. I knew that Polarfuchs was a very experienced horse and Cresta was still a novice, so I was not intending to go all out to win.

The speed and endurance day dawned hot and humid. There was not a breath of fresh air and a thundery atmosphere. Conditions were at their very worst for an arduous ride of seventeen and a half miles, including a steeplechase course two-and-a-quarter miles long with two long uphill gradients and four-and-a-half miles of cross-country over 27 obstacles.

Cresta had no idea what to expect and probably thought that phase A was a pleasant ride through the countryside, having no prior experience of the steeplechase, which was to come. We made it round so far so good and then we had to begin on the cross-country. This time I had no intention of trying to jump the post-and-rails 'hazard fence' in the middle of the lake and I took him round the long way. I had decided to take the easiest options on all of the course, particularly when a jump suddenly loomed up with hardly any warning. Cresta went very well and had only one run out, twenty penalties, when I was unable to turn him quickly enough to give him time to face the third of three angled fences. I was very pleased with him when we finished.

Next day he passed the veterinary examination with flying colours and was one of only 17 competitors left in the competition out of 34 starters. We had dropped from a close second to Polarfuchs to third behind Derek Allhusen on Laurien. We had one fence down and nine time penalties so we dropped down to fifth place but still I was pleased with him.

Chapter Twenty – True Love

After Harewood we went home, and it was time to focus on the wedding. Cresta was due to compete in the one-day events at the end of the season – Wellesbourne, Harringay, Tweseldown and Chatsworth. In the meantime, John told me that his parents had found and bought a house for us at Clitheroe, on the Lancashire-Yorkshire border. He took me to Long Acre to show me. My first impression was the house was big. It had three floors, but it was set in a plot that was narrow from left to right, hemmed in by a high beech hedge on the right and on the left boundary were a few trees linked by an anti-sheep-wire ragged fence.

We went inside, and I was knocked out. I knew that John's parents were going to buy us a house, but I hadn't expected anything as grand as this! I was sure it would be a happy home for us. The layout was all extremely well thought out and there was even a little vegetable strip and a large greenhouse, even though neither of us was going to have much time for gardening. There was also a tennis court, although neither of us were that keen on tennis. We walked to the end of the garden and looked at the wonderful view of Pendle Hill and I kissed John hard and told him I thought it was the most wonderful house for us. A rather smug smile spread all over his face.

Then becoming practical once more, I said, "But where are we going to put the horses?"

"We did think of that," he replied and turned me round to walk back through the passage and on to the entrance drive, "Over there."

He was pointing to an area which was on the left of the turning circle as one drove in from the gate. There was room for building stables, so everything would be wonderful. I was especially thrilled that I would be able to see the horses from the kitchen window. I was determined to be a wonderful housewife and would be working on my cooking skills.

The wedding invitations had gone out and we were amazed at the number of people on our list. Then Violet Clifton suggested that we hold the reception at Lytham Hall. Then I had to think about bridesmaids and a dress.I chose my new friend, Barbara Cooper, who had once traveled from London to Lytham for the series of articles in the magazine, *Illustrated*, to be Chief Bridesmaid. She liked to be called Cooper and she was an amazing person, very intelligent, and also amusing. Over the years she became immensely interested in the sport of eventing.

The other bridesmaids included Mary Whittingham, who was a dark-haired beauty with limpid brown eyes, the daughter of one of Mummy's best friends. We would be like Snow White and Rose Red! Another bridesmaid was Anne Pulham. There were three small ones: Ted and Vivian Eason's young daughter, Marian, Mrs Violet Clifton's grand-daughter, Miranda, and Jack and Marie Scott's little girl, Cynthia, who was to present the good luck charm when we stepped out of the church. I wanted an attractive bevy of females around me for the wedding.

Cooper was outstanding as a Chief Bridesmaid and she knew a wonderful dressmaker, Birghitta, who used to work in the Royal Court. I told her that I wanted a hem lifted up at the front, high rolled neck line running over my shoulders and disappearing downwards in a wide V at the back. Tiny buttons all the way down, and a trailing train.

In the meantime, I was still competing and had Cresta entered for Wellesbourne, Tweseldown and Chatsworth. Chips was also entered in the combined training class at Harringay, Horse of the Year Show as well as appearing in the Sporting Personalities from Tuesday to Saturday, every afternoon and evening. But this year I would not be staying at Dunsley.

Ted had asked me what I would like for a special wedding present and I spent a long time considering this. I told him that I had always admired the beautiful breakfast service that was used when I was staying at Dunsley. In due time a large carton arrived by carrier at Mythop Road, with complete place settings for eight, even including egg cups. It became my prized possession and was much admired at Long Acre when John and I had guests to stay and they ate their bacon and eggs off this exquisite china, and drank their coffee out of big, deep, breakfast cups.

More wonderful wedding presents arrived. Colonel Babe Moseley had always given me the impression that he found me an absolute pain on account of the Press's relentless questioning of the reason why there was a rule banning women from the Olympics eventing competition. The Press kept pointing out that I was beating the men by the largest margins ever recorded. He was very stern with me in his position as Chairman of the Selection Committee and seemed to be a stereotypical aloof army officer intent on keeping a young soldier strictly in his place.

Not until the late 1960s, did I see that beneath this front he was a real teddy bear of a man, kind and generous. He had surprised us all by marrying Kay, one of the Colman mustard family, and perhaps she was responsible for the cracking of his hard-outer shell. Whatever the reason, his wedding present showed a remarkable understanding and an acknowledgement of the partnership between Chips and myself.

He had commissioned an oil painting of Chips and me, and we were visited by Joan Wanklyn, the best equestrian painter of the time, who brought her easel and brushes on the train, set them out in the field at Lytham Hall, and made lots of sketches of us as we practised our advanced dressage work. After several days of staying with us, she returned south to paint in oils. My parents and I were bowled over by the result, which was proudly displayed on the wall of one of the rooms on the ground floor at Lytham Hall, in which all of the rest of the wedding presents were on show on big tables around the room. Joan had painted us in a dressage arena, going across the diagonal at extended trot, and in the background was Badminton House. It was a truly fantastic gift!

We received many more wonderful wedding presents, and I could not help but think, that the Waddingtons were probably very surprised by the munificence of those that came from the bride's side. I suppose this demonstrates that right from the beginning I was aware of the differing social positions of the Waddingtons and the Willcoxes.

I tried to blot out all thoughts of the impending marriage and everything that had to be done whilst I rode Cresta at Wellesbourne, where Chips was also giving a dressage display as soon as the cross-country was completed. To make matters worse, the going was deep due to very bad weather in the week before the event. In spite of adverse conditions, Cresta did well and was just beaten into second place by Jeremy Beale with his Fulmer Folly, who had been a possible for several British Event Teams. They led after the dressage, then both horses jumped clear rounds in the show jumping and over cross-country, but Cresta the novice was faster, and we moved up to a mere 0.17 point behind Jeremy. David Somerset, heir to the Duke of Beaufort, had been riding the superb Countryman for more than a year at this time and was in third place at Wellesbourne, behind Cresta. Bertie Hill had sold Countryman to the Queen and a syndicate just before Badminton in 1956, managing to enjoy the best of both worlds by pocketing a nice sum of money yet keeping the ride on his ex-horse in the Stockholm Olympics when the team won the gold medal. Sometime afterwards, Countryman became David's event horse.

The Times and Telegraph's reports on Wellesbourne were full of praise for Cresta's performance and one of them was particularly impressed: "Sheila Willcox did not have Airs and Graces going quite as well in the dressage as at Harewood, but the all-round performance was again staggering for such an inexperienced horse. It looks as if this combination may well win at Badminton next year." Reading this I hoped that they weren't going to jinx it for me. I knew that it would be an absolute miracle for Cresta to win there. On the other hand, we would be working very hard when he came in from his end of season rest in the field with Chips, and I would not be going to Badminton just to breathe in the hallowed air. But that was the future. In the present, the wedding was getting closer and there was still so much to organise.

Chatsworth was the final event of the season. It was probably my most favourite one-day event and provided proof that despite how well Cresta had done so far in his competitive life, he was still lacking in experience and was sure to make the odd mistake. I would have loved to have finished the season with a win at this last event in 1958, but we were still at the stage where I had to hold Cresta's hand round the cross-country course and give him every chance to weigh up how to jump whatever fence faced us. The Derbyshire course was boggy in patches, but that was no excuse. I knew where the going was bad and would avoid it. Cresta had shied away from the spectators during one of the movements in his dressage test. He then rolled one pole out of its cup in the show jumping, but we were still in with a chance.

Going well on the cross-country until the twelfth fence which was the drop into space coming back down the hill from Jubilee Rock, Cresta insisted on standing too far back for take-off, and caught a front leg on the top rail as he was momentarily distracted by the sight of how far below was the landing after the drop. This knocked us sideways in the air with Cresta landing half-way down and I much further on, meeting the ground nose first. I got up at once and went to Cresta who was sitting comfortably on the floor, all four legs tucked neatly underneath him, taking a breather. I told him he could not stay there and as soon as he was up we continued on around the course, blood streaming from my nose and ruining my white polo-necked sweater, splashing my plastic number.

Cresta had learnt his lesson and was intent on making no more mistakes. It says a lot for his courage that immediately after we restarted, we were facing the Ice Pond combination. He jumped straight over both these fences into the middle of the pond and finished with considerable panache. I made a great fuss of him, and we went back to our stable behind Chatsworth House where he was washed down, and thoroughly inspected for any signs of damage.

I was due to give the dressage demonstration on Chips for the crowd as the cross-country was completed. By now, Chips must have been getting fed up with all these appearances, and probably longed for the thrill of a fence in front of us to jump out of sheer joy.

I knew that after the event was over, I still had to do the right thing with Cresta. The big drop fence must be revisited, and I must show him that he could jump such a fence neatly, picking up his front legs cleanly, not just leaping into space with his eyes shut. If I left the situation as it was, then the probability would be that in the following spring, retaining bad memories of this experience, he would refuse to jump any similar fences. Having obtained permission from the organisers to return to the 'fence into space', we waited until most of the spectators had gone home and went back to it.

Cresta and I were seen climbing back up the hill as evening approached. I wouldn't be satisfied until we had jumped this fence several times. Only then would I feel that I had done my job for his future and could return to the stable to wash him down for a second time, put the cooling lotion on his legs and make him ready for the journey home. Everything that should be done, must be done, before we left Chatsworth.

The leading newspaper reporters must have still been in the Press tent when I set off up the hill and they wrote: "Miss Willcox and Airs and Graces were going well when coming up the hill from Jubilee Rock, but the horse stood back too far for the big drop (further on) at number twelve, and gave his rider a crashing fall. They finished strongly, and in the twilight were to be seen going up the hill to try that drop again – an instance of the attention to detail which has given this brilliant young horsewoman her consistent success."

The painting by Joan Wanklyn entitled "Sheila Willcox riding High and Mighty" which was given to Sheila and John as a wedding present, commissioned by Colonel Babe Mosley.

Chapter Twenty-One – Wedding Bells

It was strange to think that in only a few weeks I would be gone from Mythop Road and Lytham, and would be living with my husband John in our own house, Long Acre. Chips and Cresta were being 'roughed off', getting used to going out in the field during the day for longer and longer periods. I had arranged with a farmer down at the bottom of Standen Hey Lane, and he had assured me that the field next to Long Acre would be at my disposal

It would be the first time that I would be able to see my horses out in the field from my bedroom window. I was particularly looking forward to that. I was also looking back and remembered staying in that beautiful guest room at the Wynmalens when I could look out the window and see their manicured gardens and the fields. I was sad that there would be no more Lytham Hall which held so many happy memories, first with the ponies and the stud, then Blithe Spirit and eventing with Chips.

I had been up to London and had the first fitting for my wedding dress, but it was in such an early stage that I could not tell how it would look. The bridesmaids' frocks were nearly finished by then and the dressmaker had designed simple little caps for their hair, latticed, so that their coiffure would be hardly disturbed. By the time I went for the final fitting, on my return from Chatsworth I had taken a dislike to the wedding dress, probably for no good reason. And none of us had thought of what sort of head-dress I would be wearing. The dressmaker threw several types of veil over my head and was somewhat astonished to be told, "No I did not have a tiara." In the end she produced a fabric circlet and said that she would cover this with flowers.

I remember sitting in the train on my first-class seat and being miserable for the whole of the five-hour return journey. I was beginning to think that perhaps this marriage business was not such a good idea after all.

Next day, I had to go and join Mrs Clifton in one of the large ground floor rooms which were to be used for the wedding reception. There were family portraits of Clifton ancestors through the centuries all around the walls, and the photographer who had been sent from the local newspaper snapped away with his camera while Mrs Clifton sat regally on a large throne-like chair, her favourite whippet tucked under her left arm. I sat at her feet on a low stool, like a hand-maiden.

The day of the wedding, the 15th November, was drawing inexorably closer. The black depths of doubt which had occupied me for most of my journey back from London after the last fitting of the wedding dress, were still niggling at me. John did not notice. He was as loving as ever and kept saying how much he was looking forward to us actually being married and having me to himself.

We went to the cinema in Lytham to see Grace Kelly, Frank Sinatra and Bing Crosby in the film High Society, which had the whole nation in the thrall of Grace Kelly's beauty. John sat beside me, almost with his tongue hanging out in lust for her, as I suspect were most men in the audience, and although I laughed at him and pulled his leg, I was very hurt and the unbidden thought came into my mind – 'Ted would not have behaved like that'. Eventually Mummy registered the fact that I was not myself and asked what was wrong. I told her that I was not sure about the wedding, and I thought she was going to faint. I could see her mind running over the uproar there would be if I were to call it off. It was like looking at a cartoon character on a page with the words in a balloon caption above her head – "What about the presents? How could we tell Mrs Clifton that we would not be wanting the Hall for the reception? The food that had been ordered, the wedding presents, 250 guests to be uninvited." She sat me down and said that I really should not worry. Every girl felt like this just before the wedding. It was only natural, and I promptly burst into tears.

Perhaps I was just being silly, I thought, and I certainly did not want to do the wrong thing. I did love John, there was no doubt about that. I kept mopping away the tears until I was exhausted, and then stopped, and Mummy made us a cup of tea and deliberately put sugar in mine, in the hope of making everything better. I had not told John about my illicit relationship with Ted, which perhaps showed that we were not exceptionally close. There had been so much pressure to find a 'suitable' husband for me, and that sense of urgency created by my mother, as if the world might find out that I was spoiled goods, and no-one would want me. This marriage was without doubt, a relationship on the rebound.

The days passed, and I became more settled. The bridesmaids' frocks and head bands had arrived at each of their houses, all of them fitted perfectly and the six girls were happily looking forward to the wedding. My dress was delivered, and Mummy thought it was beautiful.

Just eight days before the wedding John had a car accident in his beloved Jaguar XK 150. A lorry had appeared, and he had taken evasive action and crashed into Cock Bridge. Luckily, no other car was involved but his car was a write-off. He was very lucky to survive, and his shoulder was strapped up, he could hardly move. He would be right for the wedding though but selfishly I thought how this would impinge on our plans for a lot of carefree and abandoned love-making.

The vast array of wedding presents was moved to the Hall so they could be displayed and we had a detective on duty twenty-four hours a day. The reception room was not wired for electricity, so Mummy had arranged for there to be candlelight.

On the morning of the wedding Mummy and Daddy came in with a breakfast tray and a red rose in a cut-glass holder. Tears came into my eyes for there was so much thought and love in this gesture. Birghitta, the dressmaker had brought my finery the day before and it was all laid out on the spare bed. Everything went to plan and outside the church were the traffic policemen and a big crowd of onlookers. The day was dull, and it had rained earlier. I got out of the car and Birghitta appeared to arrange the dress and Daddy proffered his arm and said, "Good luck, sweetheart", and we walked down the aisle to the strains of Wagner's Lohengrin. I saw Ted Marsh in the pew and smiled at him, but he made no response, staring stonily with empty eyes. Then I smiled at John as we reached the front pews and he beamed back at me. I began to feel better. A few minutes later we were husband and wife and were in the vestry signing the register.

At the reception there was a wonderful meal served in candlelight. Lytham was famous for its delicious shrimps and Joe Parkinson, coxswain of the Lytham lifeboat had gone out specially for the best shrimps he could find in the sea for the guests, 24 quarts of them. And, fresh strawberries flown in from the south of France, and 30 pounds weight of caviar, a marvellous cake four tiers high and weighing more than 100 pounds, 480 bottles of champagne. No one could have done more for a daughter and I was utterly entranced that my parents had supplied such a wedding for us.

<blockquote>
Now it was simply a matter of

living the 'happily ever after'
</blockquote>

Printed in Great Britain
by Amazon